SEVEN LITERARY ANTITHEISTS

SEVEN LITERARY ANTITHEISTS

from Diderot to Beckett

DAVID GORDON

EYECORNER PRESS

© DAVID GORDON & EyeCorner Press | 2013

SEVEN LITERARY ANTITHEISTS
from Diderot to Beckett

Published by EYECORNER PRESS
February 2013
Roskilde

ISBN: 978-87-92633-22-4

Cover design and layout: Camelia Elias

Printed in the US and UK

CONTENTS

Introduction: What is Literary Antitheism? / 7

1. The Pre-Revolutionary Antitheism of Denis Diderot / 11

2. The Post-Revolutionary Antitheism of Georg Büchner / 25

3. The Metatheism of Friedrich Nietzsche / 35

4. Mark Twain's Countertheology / 51

5. The Poetry of Doubt: Thomas Hardy's Antitheism / 65

6. The Elegant Antitheism of Wallace Stevens / 77

7. Samuel Beckett and the Bastard Who Doesn't Exist / 87

Bibliography / 98

INTRODUCTION

What is Literary Antitheism?

I start from the assumption that the question of whether God exists is tiresome because it is badly framed. Anyone likely to be reading this book would take for granted that a factual claim for a supernatural intelligence concerned in some fashion with humankind cannot be maintained. But that hardly settles the matter. If we pay attention to the ways emotive language is actually used, we must recognize that the idea of such divine existence, typically denoted by the word God, continues to play a part in the imaginative life of writers and readers at all levels of sophistication. It persists in the minds not only of those who feel friendly to the idea of God but also in the minds of those who do not.

The most important shift in the modern history of the God question occurred during the eighteenth century Enlightenment and is encapsulated in Immanuel Kant's statement: "God is not a being outside me, but merely a thought in me." That inward turn has enabled post-Enlightenment theists to argue persuasively that a belief in divine existence is a deep-seated conviction and therefore cannot be dismissed on rational grounds. But, although this inward turn warrants a psychologically based theism, it does not explain why the idea remains resonant in modern literary culture, even among those writers and readers advanced enough to dismiss quietly any factual claim of divine existence. My interest in the following pages does not extend to any of the noisy, self-declared "atheists" from whom we have heard enough in recent years. It is devoted rather to the work of writers I am calling "antitheists," subtle imaginers who oppose the strength of an idea that they find lodged *in their own minds.*

I suggest that we call this persistent God-idea, powerful to poets as well as to religious believers, *myth*. Although the word myth in our day is often used pejoratively, referring to *false* belief-narratives, it is also used to describe aesthetically compelling ones wherein the question or truth or falsity is not at issue. And this latter meaning is well established and valued particularly by those with a literary education. Many poems, plays, novels, and even essays gain their strength from the felt presence of some myth or combination of myths. Indeed, inspired writers may sometimes, without knowing it, tap into the resonance of a mythic narrative and thereby more deeply engage their readers.

Key quotations from two major twentieth-century poets will clarify what work I am asking the phrase "deeply engage" to do here. T. S. Eliot, commenting on religious poetry, wrote: "the poet never persuades us to believe anything.... What we learn from religious poetry is what it feels like to believe that religion." Eliot here implies a distinction between two kinds of thinking in language, ratiocinative thought serving what might broadly be called political ends, on the one hand, and, on the other, intimate, imaginative thought serving aesthetic ends. A quotation from W. B. Yeats offers an important supplement to Eliot's distinction: "We make out of the quarrel with others, rhetoric, but of the quarrel with ourselves, poetry." This quotation suggests that, although political and poetic language may both reflect strong feeling, the expressed feeling in the second case will be more mobile, more self-critical, more conflicted, more likely to take a dialogic and ironic form.

For some of the uses to which the word God has been put (such as abstract, philosophical reasoning) the word "myth" does not seem to be a very precise description. I should therefore add that, although Nietzsche and Stevens occasionally use the word in such a way (to signify the fundamental human ability to create coherent, imaginative meaning), all of my literary antitheists, including these two, are dealing primarily with anthropomorphic ideas of deity, and therefore with indubitable myths.

The careers of the seven writers under consideration span Western intellectual history from the mid-eighteenth to the mid-twentieth century. A little explanation is called for both as to why I gather close analyses of individual sensibilities into a historically organized account and why I have chosen these particular seven writers from a larger pool. The historical dimension is important because major scientific and political developments during these two centuries reframed questions concerning God and religion and inevitably influenced individual orientations to these questions. And my choice of these seven, although not inevitable, does allow me to represent pretty well subsequent phases in the history of ideas over this period. Diderot and Büchner exemplify respectively pre-and post-Revolutionary literary antitheism, the one more intellectually speculative, the other more emotionally desperate. Nietzsche undertakes a psycho-historical analysis of theology and meets the challenge both to religion and art resulting from the new prestige of science. Twain and Hardy illustrate in different ways the quarrel with God that we find at the end of the Victorian era, Twain by way of extravagant satire, Hardy by way of brooding on the lack of fitness between man and the cosmos. Stevens speaks for an age in which religious doubt has ceased to be troubling yet the need to believe remains. And Beckett's post-World War II probe of nothingness rejects hopeful belief yet creates out of the very absence of meaning an art of extraordinary invention.

A history of ideas is richer, I think, if we start from the complex consciousness of individual writers and work outward toward wider developments and tendencies, rather than the other way around. This procedure enables us to honor a sense of depth (in my view the sine qua non of good criticism) while reaching also for a valuable sense of breadth.

The Pre-Revolutionary Antitheism of Denis Diderot

The belief that only natural causes operated in the material world was the leading issue of the antitheistic discourse in Western Europe that was gradually gaining strength during the seventeenth and eighteenth centuries. Diderot embraced this belief, but his style of thinking was dramatic and playful. Frequently it was inflected with irony in order to mislead the suspicious and malicious agents of Church and State. Moreover, he was too much the moralist to be content with merely a skeptical line of thought. He wanted to explain *why* all of nature was ever changing and especially *why* human beings, who were part of this material world, found themselves so concerned with ethical questions like the meaning of virtue and the freedom of moral choice.

Diderot's commitment to materialism emerged rapidly in three works composed in his mid-thirties, from 1746 to 1749, and an inclination to play with ideas is already noticeable in them. *Pensées philosophiques* was influenced by the Earl of Shaftesbury's deistic *Inquiry Concerning Virtue and Merit* a treatise that Diderot, at first impressed by the idea that moral sentiment depended on belief in God, had translated and introduced a year earlier. But he carried the inquiry beyond deism in order to challenge to Pascal's fideistic *Pensées*. Although the work mixed together deistic and skeptical viewpoints, the latter have a sharper edge, as in this epigrammatic flourish: "The thought that there is no God has never frightened anyone; what is frightening is the thought that there might be one, of the kind that people describe." *The Skeptic's Stroll* balances deistic against atheistic surmise, officially honoring the first while inclining to the second. A more substantial piece, *Letter on the Blind, For the Use of Those Who See*, shows us a blind mathematician whose inability to appreciate the argument from design—and by extension any kind of theism—is a lesson for the sighted, teaching that they cannot know any more than the blind about the deity. Reminding his sighted interlocutor that an Indian believes the globe remains suspended in the air because it is borne on the back of an elephant that rests on a tortoise, etc., the blind man enjoins him to "confess your ignorance right away, and spare me the elephant and the tortoise."[1]

The authorities burned *Philosophical Thoughts* (although a copy was printed and became rather popular), searched Diderot's lodging and carried off *The Skeptic's Stroll*, warning the author not to write anything else against religion. But Diderot went ahead with the bolder *Letter on the Blind*, and sent a copy to Voltaire, France's leading man of letters at mid-century but known to be, despite his anti-clericalism and distaste for theology, a deist. In fact, Voltaire was somewhat disturbed by it, replying that "it is quite impertinent to guess what [God] is or why he made the

---

1   For a good introduction to Diderot's thoughts concerning materialism (and its antitheistic implications), see: Crocker (ed.), *Diderot's Selected Writings*; Stewart and Kemp (eds.), *Diderot: Interpreter of Nature*: and, most fully, his dialogue, *D'Alembert's Dream*. That dialogue wrestles bravely with the bearing of recent research in anatomy, physiology and medicine on the big question of why anything exists and to what end—without falling back on religious beliefs.

world, but it seems to me very bold to deny that he exists." Diderot's reply bends over backward to be tactful, without surrendering its main point, the unimportance of believing in God. "It is very important," he remarks with jaunty, irrepressible wit, "not to confuse hemlock with parsley, but not important at all to believe or not to believe in God."[2]

Not long after the publication of *Letter on the Blind*, Diderot was seized and put into prison for a few months, an experience that made him more prudent and canny, but not more compromising, in the service of truth. He submitted his work to the authorities when he could, withheld much of it from publication in his lifetime, and threw himself into the huge and extended enterprise of the *Encyclopedia*, which, though an object of suspicion and several kinds of censorship, was also a source of pride to France and enjoyed the support of some people of influence. At times Diderot clothed what he wrote in deadpan irony in order to deceive naïve readers while getting his subversive point across to more knowing ones, as in this passage from *The Interpretation of Nature*: "Religion spares us many errors and much labor. If it had not enlightened us on the origin of the world, how many different hypotheses should we have been tempted to take for nature's secret." The "If" clause seems to concede ultimate truth to the Church, making the subversive point of the statement more difficult to detect and penalize.

Diderot's nimbleness, then, was sometimes aroused by circumstances, but it was also characteristic, and led him to bring to the speculative essay a striking dialogic art. From the beginning, even in works not formally in dialogue, his habit was to oppose one opinion to another, and this underwent development in such

---

2 Diderot, "*Correspondance 1713-1757*," pp. 74-78.

mature works as *Rameau's Nephew* and *D'Alembert's Dream*. In the first of these, it isn't just a question of balancing *Moi* against *Lui* in vigorous debate. Yes, *Moi* represents a side of Diderot, the bourgeois man of good sense and good will, but the characteristic mobility of the writer's mind is mostly represented by *Lui*, the nephew, who takes over and dizzies us with telling subversions of conventional moral assumptions. About "D'Alembert's Dream" Diderot boasted to his friend and confidante Sophie Vallon: "It is the height of extravagance but at the same time the most profound philosophy. It is quite cunning of me to have put my ideas in the mouth of a dreamer. You often have to dress up wisdom as folly in order to gain admittance for it."[3] Persons named Diderot and D'Alembert are debating materialism one evening, and the more conservative D'Alembert in his sleep then carries Diderot's thoughts even farther, which, overheard, are interpreted for our benefit by a Diderot stand-in to a charming but mystified young lady, Julie de L'Espinasse, in real life a close friend of D'Alembert's. In both dialogues the writer is less interested in driving at firm conclusions than in the pleasure of speculation itself.

Diderot liked to call himself "the philosopher," a word that meant for him someone committed to the endlessly fascinating art of inquiry, neither the systematic skepticism of Hume on the one hand nor the dogmatic materialism of La Mettrie, Holbach and Helvétius on the other. His model inquirer was Montaigne, whose grand art is that he "never tries to prove (*prouver*) but is always experimenting (*prouvant*)."[4] Diderot might well be called a rambunctious version of Montaigne, full of strong opinions sharply expressed but always wary of dogmatism. His postscript

---

3 Quoted in Stott, *Darwin's Ghosts*, p. 149.
4 Cited by Sherman, *Diderot*, p. 53.

to *The Interpretation of Nature* sums up his stance with admirable concision: "Never forget that *nature* is not *God*, that a *man* is not a *machine*, that a *hypothesis* is not a *fact*." Both deists and overly enthusiastic materialists, like his friend Baron Holbach, were apt to confuse nature and God, La Mettrie and Helvétius to confuse man and machine, and the naturalists of his day to confuse hypothesis and fact. Unlike the dogmatic atheist, Diderot would allow room for a play of perspective, and thus for a potential humanism to emerge even out of a deterministic base.

Diderot's most thorough analyses of materialism's implications are found in *The Interpretation of Nature* (1753) and in *D'Alembert's Dream* (1769). Drawing on Descartes, Bacon and Newton, and carrying their thinking a step or two farther, this philosopher made a serious effort to show that matter was not merely inert. *Ame* was not to be understood as either opposed to *corps* or behind it, but inseparable from it. He was working out a dynamic materialism, and one of his critics provides in this connection helpful background to indicate that mid-eighteenth century European speculation was moving away from a mechanical view of nature based on astronomy and physics and moving toward a dynamic view based on biology, physiology and chemistry.[5] Diderot, alert to these developments, defended the bold new idea that nature was not stable or fixed but always evolving. His science is of course now antiquated, but it is nonetheless surprising to see how far he was able to go in understanding change, development, growth, even evolution, without any knowledge of Darwin. For him there could be no essential distinction between humans and other animals if the basic fact of all life was change and development, although such a belief was highly offensive to

---

5   John Hope Mason, *The Irresistible Diderot*, p. 12.

the Church. And he exercised a good deal of ingenuity in speculating on the interaction of organic and inorganic matter. To be sure, he was obliging himself down the line to explain what *was* distinctive in man, but his dynamic materialism in itself retained appeal for some even into the nineteenth century, like Karl Marx who also wanted to account for the dynamic nature of nature without recourse to a supreme intelligence. Rebecca Stott's recent book, *Darwin's Ghosts*, establishes his credentials as an important contributor to the evolutionary speculation that led up to the epochal theory of natural selection.[6]

Since Diderot was at bottom not what we would call a scientist but a moralist, his greatest challenge as speculator was to account for the moral dimension in man. How could one explain morality if behavior is ruled by material processes beyond our conscious control? And if Diderot was a determinist (though that word did not come into use until the nineteenth century—the word "necessity" being its earlier equivalent), in what sense was he also a humanist? One book about him is divided into two parts, one about his materialism and the other his humanism.[7] Another labels him "a dualist in spite of himself."[8] Both labels make sense but I recommend "perspectivist," which highlights the way his supple intellect moves flexibly between contrasting points of view.

Diderot first seriously engaged the problem of fitting together material and moral man in the so-called "Letter to Landois," pursued the problem in *Refutation of a Work Entitled 'On Man' by*

---

6 Stott, Chap. 7.
7 Willa Anderson, *Diderot's Dream*.
8 Aram Vartanian, in *Diderot: A Bicentennial Tribute*.

Helvétius, and rounded out his view (implicitly) in the novel *Jacques the Fatalist and His Master*.

Landois was an earnest but untalented writer who, having contributed a few articles to the *Encyclopedia*, then wrote an angry letter to Diderot in 1756 about slow payment, lack of comment on his work, and the malignant way in which he was treated by the world in general. According to P. N. Furbank, whose excellent pages on the subject I draw upon,[9] the Landois letter, though it has not survived, probably made jibes at the hypocrisy of its editor's interest in virtue. Seeing an occasion for a clarifying statement of principle, Diderot wrote an important rejoinder, which may never have been sent but was published by his friend Grimm and is known as the "Letter to Landois". It explained that our moral faculty is not opposed to the passions (the traditional view) but only helps us choose among them. We do everything for our own sake, but this is obscured by the fact that we have conflicting desires. We do not choose our desires themselves, we cannot want to want, and so the act of choosing among them becomes "a banal little event" (as he pointed out in the article on Will in the *Encyclopedia*). But we think we have free (undetermined) will because we are aware of willing.

As early as *Philosophical Thoughts* Diderot sought to honor both virtue and the passions, but hadn't coordinated them. Here he attempts to do so, and so I will amplify Furbank's account by noting that this coordination anticipates some noteworthy later thinking. Kant, for example, remarked in the *Critique of Practical Reason* that it is possible to regard the same psychological event as being either an effect of nature or the result of freedom. And

---

9   Furbank, *Diderot: A Critical Biography*, pp. 135-38.

the contemporary biologist E. O. Wilson wrote in his influential book *Consilience* that, although freedom of the will is an illusion, we believe in it because of our conscious effort (given our partial ignorance of the determining causes) in choosing.

E. O. Wilson's view, be it noted, is not quite perspectival in my sense of the word because it comes at the problem only from the scientific point of view, never entering, as the literary man does, into the subjective world of the chooser. Diderot would have understood what Wilson calls the "unity of knowledge" more flexibly, ready as he always was to move between a scientific and a humanistic point of view. As he commented neatly in "Elements of Physiology," "man is both a book and the reader of that book." Shuttling between these perspectives was basic to his thinking. Addressing the same problem, Kant described it as "the antinomy of freedom." And Nietzsche, that consummate perspectivist, similarly distinguished between freedom spontaneously experienced and the intellect's knowledge that everything is causally determined; our living, in his view, requires this freedom, but analysis cannot grasp it.

Diderot returned to the issue of free will when he had to explain what was unsatisfactory about the reductive determinism of Helvétius' treatise *De L'Homme*, which he read and re-read during the 1770s, not because of its intrinsic merit but because of the direct way it challenged him to articulate a broader view of human nature. For Helvétius, all human behavior was the result of sensation and environment. His was a purely quantitative theory of self-interest that anticipates in some respects Jeremy Bentham's calculus of pleasure and pain, and Diderot's response, as Arthur M. Wilson suggests, resembles J. M. Mill's response to

Bentham.[10] Diderot did not wish to dispute the issue of determinism as such and thereby abandon the materialist hypothesis, but he believed that Helvétius left too much out. Men act as well as react, judge as well as feel, find pleasure in doing and thinking as well as in sensing. For Helvétius people were interchangeable counters, as if (Diderot said nicely) he had never observed children. For Diderot, people were not only different from one another but their minds were plastic, modifiable by education. He judged people to be agents as well as objects, readers of the book as well as the book itself. Helvétius' ideas did strengthen Diderot's humanism, but we should remember that his humanism and materialism sometimes clashed, in which case they could only be coordinated with irony. Which brings us to *Jacques the Fatalist*.

Quoting some of the first page or two will provide a basis for pertinent commentary:[11]

> How did they meet? By chance like everyone else. What were their names? What's that got to do with you? Where were they coming from? From the nearest place. Where were they going to? Does anyone really know where they are going to? What were they saying? The master wasn't saying anything and Jacques was saying that his Captain used to say that everything that happens on this earth [*ici-bas*], both good and bad, is written up above [*là-haut*]....
>
> *The Master.* And you stopped the bullet with your name on it.
>
> *Jacques,* You've guessed it. Shot in the knee. And God knows the good and bad fortunes brought about by that shot....

---

10 Wilson, *Diderot*, p. 666.
11 Diderot, *Jacques the Fatalist and His Master*, pp. 21-22.

> So you can see, Reader, that I am well away, and that it's entirely within my power to make you wait a year, or two, or even three years for the story of Jacques' loves, by separating him from his master and exposing each of them to whatever perils I liked.

The Diderot scholar Aram Vartanian observed that "Jacques *acts* on the assumption of freedom, but theorizes on the assumption of necessity."[12] That difference does indeed lead us directly to the book's essential complication, and could be developed, for the narrator handles the reader much the way Jacques handles his master (whom he will overturn in the narrative). One could say of the narrator that, like Jacques, he acts on the assumption of freedom and theorizes on the assumption of chance. In this mock novel, strongly influenced by Laurence Sterne, Necessity (or fatalism) and Chance (or freedom) are linked as metaphysical forces that rule our lives. It is sometimes said that the novel mocks Spinoza's universe, but in Spinoza freedom is ultimately one with necessity whereas Diderot wants to dramatize the ironic tension between them, between the belief that we are able to choose and the belief that choice is already determined.

The notion of fatalism in the novel is too often associated with determinism, an awkward association since Diderot didn't have the word and an inaccurate one as well. To be a fatalist (in this case) is to believe that all our actions here on earth are compelled by forces above and beyond us and thus to make a mockery of freedom, as Jacques does in the quoted passage. But to be a determinist for Diderot (and scientists today) is to believe merely that every event has a material cause. Such a belief does not prevent our ability to act on the assumption of freedom and to value

---

[12] Cited by Otis Fellows, *Diderot*, p. 126.

that assumption, even if, from a strictly materialistic point of view, it is an illusion. The "Letter to Landois" sought to demonstrate logically that morality was not opposed to the involuntary passions. "The Refutation" argued that complex human beings think and act as subjects and not merely as objects. And *Jacques the Fatalist* turns away from philosophical arguing to literary showing, presenting with nimble wit the ironic comedy of the two perspectives clashing—and clashing four times over: within Jacques, within the narrator, in the relation between Jacques and his master, in the relation between narrator an reader.

For the 1772 New Year celebration at Baron Holbach's house, Diderot composed satiric verse, as he had on two previous anniversaries, for the private pleasure of his friends. On this occasion his elaborate piece (entitled *Les Eleuthéromanes*, "Maniacs for freedom") adopted a classic verse form that licensed anger, probably because Louis XV had just angered a number of libertarians by stripping *Parlement* of its authority and thus taking a serious step toward tyranny. One inflammatory distich in Diderot's festive ode ("And for want of a rope his hands will knot/ The guts of the priest to strangle kings") had the misfortune of being published in 1795, after his death, and, according to Furbank, "it was seized on with outraged zest by the enemies of the Revolution, and for many years afterwards would earn Diderot a reputation as an arch Jacobin."[13]

I make a point of this because, while Diderot was certainly libertarian and egalitarian in his political sympathies, he was not a revolutionary, and this fact contributes to the complexity of his overall thinking. Impulsive as he was, he also had a realistic sense of what could be done and even what prudently should be done

---

13 Furbank, pp. 354-66.

in view of the superior power of state and church. This is clearly evident in two of his shorter dialogic works, "Conversations of a Father with his Children" and "Conversations with a Christian lady." In the first, "Denis" grows indignant at a manifestly unjust law which (he feels) ought to be disobeyed, but the last word is given to the kindly father who is pleased that someone is around who thinks as his son does but also relieved that there are not many such around, potential subverters of government. In the second, the figure standing in for Diderot demonstrates to a charming titled lady that the religious instruction she relies on for moral guidance is purely conventional, and not at all a necessary support for the morality of her behavior, but when she finally turns to ask whether *he* would tell the truth about his irreligion before magistrates or would receive last rites when near death, he says he would compromise his principles, an untroubled hypocrite. The tone throughout their conversation is gallant and gracious, a little testament to the highly civilized discourse possible in the days of the *ancien régime*.

It is remarkable that the pre-Revolutionary antitheism of Diderot, even allowing for his uniqueness, should be relatively free of doubt and anguish, compared to the agonized religious doubting that we find throughout the nineteenth century. Various reasons for this difference have been offered and I want to touch on two of them. One is that most of the *philosophes* were able to believe in progress, aware of dramatic gains already made and sensing that the very oppressiveness of the Monarchy and the Church made their power vulnerable to further modification. (The violence of the Revolution and of its reactionary aftermath they could, of course, not foresee.) The other is that they were ignorant also of the breadth and depth of the intellectually revolutionary "inward turn" that would follow in its wake, driving the deity out of the heavens and reinstating him within the human mind where he was more difficult to dislodge. Diderot, for all his sophistication, was free of the sort of self-consciousness that would burden, among many others, Büchner, Nietzsche, Twain, and Hardy.

The Post-Revolutionary Antitheism
of Georg Büchner

Büchner too embraced materialism and wrestled with the deterministic moral philosophy it entailed, a struggle complicated by the fact that, unlike Diderot, he was also a passionate revolutionary. He was keenly disappointed by the collapse of the French Revolution's ideals, and tried hard in his short, intense life (1813-1837) to organize a Society for the Rights of Man. But after his efforts to overthrow the Hessian regime nearly led to imprisonment, his outlook came to be pervaded by a sense of historical necessity and of man's helplessness in the face of it. He rejected the Enlightenment's faith in reason, along with the deism that had at first attracted him in the writing of Voltaire. He quickly became too bitter for an accommodating view of the God question. In his small oeuvre,[1] the central theme is that a God who could bear to watch over man's senseless suffering is intolerable.

On the basis of his study of the French Revolution, he could find no hope for mankind arising from historical change. Despite

---

[1] It includes, along with some letters, three dramatic works (*Danton's Death, Leonce and Lena, Woyzeck*), one pamphlet (*The Hessian Messenger*) and a story (*Lenz*). All my quotations from his masterpiece, *Danton's Death*, are based on the Oxford University Press edition.

their high reputation in German thought at the time, he rejected the idealist historiographies of Hegel and Fichte, and, had he not died so young, he probably would also have opposed Marx's utopianism because he could no longer believe in a human *will to rebel*. While working on *Danton's Death* he wrote in an often-quoted letter: "[Studying the Revolution] I find a terrible uniformity in human nature, an inexorable force conferred upon all and none, in human circumstances. The individual: mere foam on the wave, greatness pure chance, the mastery of genius a puppet play, a ridiculous struggle against an iron law to acknowledge which is the highest good, to defeat impossible."[2]

This suggests the antiheroic nature of the work being composed, but its author is too angry for mere resignation. The letter goes on to find the word "must" that appears to govern human history and human psychology a "damned word." Büchner's first work, a pamphlet called "The Hessian Messenger" (although toned down by his collaborator) sounds like a mixture of biblical jeremiad and the screeds of the young Shelley directed at the reactionaries of England. One reason, doubtless, why his great play is set in the midst of the Revolution is that some of this political ardor can be appropriately expressed, even though it is ardor dampened by an underlying conviction of human helplessness.

Büchner was a serious scientist as well as writer, working in medicine and biology, and he represented his characters with clinical precision and objectivity, but, in doing so, he could not suppress a cry of pain. This contradiction helps to account for the extraordinary tension that critics find in his work and for the adjectives they regularly use to describe it—powerful, relentless, inexorable, passionate, personal, bitter, and the like.

---

2   Quoted by Carl Mueller (ed.), *Büchner: Complete Plays and Prose*, p. xv.

Critical description of Danton's Death as anti-heroic is certainly apt, and has been well developed by Herbert Lindenberger, who subtitles a chapter on the play "Antirhetoric and Dramatic Form," and by Victor Brombert, who discusses the play in a book titled In Praise of Antiheroes.3 Danton himself is of course the central antihero, a character, who returns throughout the play to the idea that life is "essentially a series of games which we play to pass our time away and to remind us as rarely as possible of the great emptiness that stares at us from behind the surfaces of things." Lindenberger offers that assessment, and is particularly perceptive in contrasting Danton's natural tone and lively sense of metaphor to Robespierre's cliché-ridden deadness of language and tendency to use abstractions like Vice and Virtue. But we should notice also that, if not a hero of action, Danton is in fact a hero of insight. There is little progressive movement in the play, but Danton, though doomed (as the title implies), begins with a margin of hope and gradually achieves, as he approaches death, a fuller realization of "the iron law" of history. He is someone who can acknowledge this law, and is the only character allowed a glimpse of the future, of the condemnation of Robespierre himself and of the dictatorship to follow. Finally he realizes that even death will not bring peace: "If the greatest peace of all is God, doesn't it follow that nothingness is God? But I'm an atheist. That damned argument: something cannot become nothing, there's the misery."

We will return to this curious and interesting theology presently, but first it is important to understand that the character given the name of Thomas Paine is also a hero of insight, linked

---

3   Lindenberger, *Georg Büchner: Modern Critiques*. Brombert, *In Praise of Antiheroes*.

to Danton not only in terms of patriotism (Danton says to him, "What you did for the good of your country I tried to do for mine") but also as an "epicurean." He explains in terms of this philosophy how people can be imagined as both determined by their natures yet intellectually heroic as well. In the one long scene in which he appears, he is a sympathetic figure whose views are not much different from Danton's own. Some critics[4] stress a contrast between Paine and Danton, the one dogmatic and earnest, the other beyond all that. But that contrast seems to me less important than it appears to be. Precisely because Danton cannot expatiate on his views without becoming less convincing as the central character of a *drama,* Büchner needs someone like Paine to fill in the conceptual underpinning. Nor is Paine quite a dogmatist. His first few speeches (delivered to Chaumette, nicknamed Anaxagoras because he claims to be an atheist) are indeed catechistic in form and dogmatic in tone, but we soon discover that Paine is in this way *mocking* the pedantry of theological speculation in order to demonstrate that falling back on reason doesn't work. You cannot, he says, "explain an imperfect effect proceeding from a perfect cause….[Voltaire did so only because] he didn't dare break with gods any more than with kings." Once this intent is made clear to us, Paine speaks not only passionately but with his author's implicit endorsement:

> Why go through that rigmarole [i.e. the ingenuities of theological argument] just to make ourselves out the sons of God? I prefer a lesser father; at least I can't reproach him with educating me beneath my station, in a pigsty or in the galleys. Do away with imperfection; that's the only way you'll prove the existence of God. Spinoza tried it. We can deny evil but not pain. Only rea-

---

4   For example, Ronald Hauser.

son can prove God. The senses reject Him. Take note, Anaxagoras, Why do I suffer? That is the rock of my atheism. The least twinge of pain, should it convulse a single atom, splits creation from top to bottom.

It is of little importance that the historical Paine himself was a deist, not an atheist. Büchner is getting at something original and impressive here. Theodicies like Milton's *Paradise Lost* and Pope's *Essay on Man* understood pain and suffering as part of the evil of life that a more complete understanding of divine will would justify. But Büchner pointedly distinguished pain (*Schmerz*) and suffering (*Leid*) from evil (*Böse*). While evil can be explained as the result of imperfect human understanding, and was so explained by Christian theologians and (in a different way) by Spinoza, pain and suffering derive from our very existence as physical bodies, and so, for Büchner, can never be justified. They cry out that the world we inhabit is forever imperfect. Even the cynical Laflotte in *Danton's Death*, ready to betray the prisoners, endorses in an aside the Paine-Danton-Büchner view that turns away from both the Christian and Spinozistic rationales: "pain is the only sin and suffering the only vice." A political solution to the problem of pain is implied to be sure, but it is too utopian to be more than another cry of pain: do away with imperfection, and then we can call ourselves children of God.

How is so intensely moral a position compatible with a deterministic philosophy that belittles freedom of the will? A further speech of Paine's shows how this question is addressed: "First you prove God from morality and then morality from God! What's the point of your morality? I don't know whether there's anything good or bad *per se*. I don't have to change my way of life on that account. I act according to my nature. What suits it is good for me, and I do it. What's contrary to it is bad for me, and I don't do it." By means of this sort of epicurean reasoning, which seems to make authentic moral behavior the exclusive province of the spontaneous natural man, Büchner does find a way, albeit a marginal way, to bring together morality and a deterministic philosophy.

In the play, it is of course Danton who combines the two aspects most fully. He is the epicurean natural man and he expresses a deterministic position with most dramatic authority. We see this clearly in the way he confronts Robespierre, the disciple of Rousseau and apostle of Virtue, known as the Incorruptible. Throughout the play Robespierre talks of virtue and vice, one crushing the other, apart from actual people and their feelings. Here is the key exchange between him and Danton, an exchange that broadens the moral dimension by connecting Christ with (fine) epicureanism and thus with the admirable, altogether human antiheroism of Danton:

ROBESPIERRE: You deny the existence of virtue?

DANTON: And of vice. There are only Epicureans, coarse ones and fine ones. Christ was the finest. That's the only difference between men that I've been able to discover. Everyone acts according to his nature—in other words he does what does him good.

Christ as exemplary Epicurean obeys the law of *his* nature, and Danton identifies himself with this idea of Christ. It is true that Robespierre also identifies himself with Christ--"the Son of Man...crucified in all of us [as we] writhe in bloody sweat in the Garden of Gethsemane"--and wonders as well if we control our own actions. But *his* words are pompous, reflecting less genuine feeling, We may note that there are more genuinely troubled protagonists elsewhere in Büchner who are also identified with Christ—Woyzeck for one and also Lenz who at one point in his anguish tries, but fails, to raise a child from the dead.

The play is set in the spring of 1794 when the Terror reigned. Danton had helped to bring about the present situation but is now disillusioned, even fatalistic about what will come, though also, in spurts, ironic or indignant. When the play finally found its audience fifty years after Büchner's death (thanks to the Naturalistic movement in German drama led by Gerhard Hauptmann), two of its features required some adjustment of expectations. One was the collage-like arrangement of scenes that did not seem to constitute a plot with a rising and falling action. The other was the passivity of the protagonist. Audiences were being asked to understand that Danton's role was not to act in some consequential way but to think about death or, more exactly, to reflect on a philosophical conundrum—why does anything exist? Diderot rather enjoyed the fact that philosophers were embarrassed by this conundrum and suggested puckishly that only revelation could answer it.[5] Büchner took it seriously but came at it in an unusual way, asking how something, the created world, can turn into nothing. And if it cannot, if there is no nothingness, then the created world is a wound, a perpetual hopelessness and so may be called a perpetual severance from God. Indeed the intensity of his pity seems to spring from his perception that human beings are forever deprived of God. Maurice Benn commented: "If [men] were creatures of God there would be hope for them; but they appear to [Büchner] like lost children, without a father

---

5 Crocker (ed.), *Diderot*, p. 87.

and without hope—and it is precisely the hopelessness that inflames his pity."⁶

Danton is the character who broods most on decomposition and decay, on the subversion of any political hope for man by the very meaninglessness of the universe. He is passive without being a static characterization. He speaks of boredom without being boring. The charm of the natural man, touched by a sense of futility, is expressed through his relations with women and friends. The objectivity with which he and other characters are presented does not come across as coldness because, while there is little conventional sentiment bestowed on individuals, much pity is bestowed, through their speeches, upon the human situation itself. Büchner describes his attitude toward his creations in terms of laughter of a peculiarly purgative kind: "my laughter is not at how a human being is but rather at the fact *that* he is a human being; about which he can do nothing; and at the same time laugh at myself because I must share in his fate."⁷

He liked to discover his characters in extreme states and situations, often near or in a state of madness. While the major characters manage to maintain a hold on sanity, Danton's friend Camille Desmoulins is driven very near madness when condemned to death, and his wife Lucille is driven *over* the edge. Danton's wife Julie, contrary to the historical record (she remarried and outlived even Büchner) commits suicide in one brief but strong scene. Beyond this play, Woyzeck's half-madness is memorable (thanks in part to Alban Berg's opera) and J. M. R. Lenz (the Storm and Stress poet with whom Büchner clearly identified) draws back from his madness only after much anguish.

---

6   Maurice Benn, *The Drama of Revolt*, p. 70.
7   Letter of 1834, quoted in Mueller (ed.), p. xvi.

In this author's work, the madness of men finds its counterpart in the impotence of God, and his sense of that impotence is acute, experienced with extraordinary keenness. In Michael Hamburger's words, "Wherever atheism occurs in his work...it is as revolt, experienced with an intensity that can be described as religious."[8] Although this doesn't exactly make Büchner a believer, at least in any customary sense, it does throw light on his remarkable deathbed utterance: "We do not suffer too much pain, indeed we suffer too little, for through our pain we are brought nearer to God."[9] Perhaps deathbed words somewhat at odds with the drift of one's work should not be emphasized, but in fact these words do illuminate aspects of that work. For to say that pain is the rock of one's atheism is also to imply that it is in the most extreme state that one is most aware of God's terrible absence. Büchner is identifying his own extraordinary pity with the unrealized pity of God. On his author's behalf surely, Lenz spoke these words, which were found blasphemous by his pastor-friend: "If I were almighty, if I were that, I could not endure this suffering; I would save Man from it, save him. All I ask is rest, rest, just a little rest."

A better label than "blasphemy" or even atheism for this stance is anguished antitheism. Büchner cannot do without the "Almighty" because he needs to account in some non-abstract way for the utter pitiableness of the human situation. And he must finally condemn Him because he cannot distinguish the Almighty's radical impotence from his own anguished sense of human helplessness.

---

8   Hamburger (ed.), p. xii.
9   Quoted by Lindenberger, p. 15.

The Metatheism of Friedrich Nietzsche

The books known to have influenced Nietzsche in his youth included materialist and skeptical classics like *Force and Matter* by Ludwig Büchner (Georg's brother), *History of Materialism* by F. A. Lange, Feuerbach's *Essence of Christianity,* and D. F. Strauss's *Life of Jesus Critically Examined.* He soon turned from theology (his father had been a Lutheran pastor) to classical philology and then to philosophy. We know that what attracted him most in Schopenhauer, his chief precursor in the philosophical work he was to undertake, was not only the assumption of atheism with its accompanying materialist bias but also the psychological interest in the will, which would lead him to probe extensively the *motives* of religious belief. Like Freud after him, Nietzsche achieved some of his keenest insights in asking not *what* people believed but *why.* Yet his temper was enthusiastic as well as critical, positive as well as skeptical. Although he was too independent to accept the beliefs of others, including the beliefs cherished by the religion he grew up with, he himself sought to relocate the spirit that went into religion in the volatile spirit of creativity itself.

The principal agent that jolted Nietzsche into the kind of oppositional stance we regard as characteristic of him was, I think, Darwin. His acceptance of Darwin's naturalism was profound, but this is not apparent because his cast of mind protested against thinking of individuals, especially gifted ones, in terms of mass behavior. For Darwin, progress was measured by the success of species rather than of individuals whereas for Nietzsche "the feeling of being STRONGER, quite aside from its usefulness in the struggle [with others], is the real progress: it is from this feeling that the will to struggle first arises."[1] Nonetheless, it was the premise of man-beast kinship on which he pivoted to explain this will to struggle. In the essay "History in the Service and Disservice of Life" (published in a volume titled *Unmodern Observations*), he acknowledged that human beings are also animals, and added, crucially, the following contrast: beasts live "unhistorically" whereas human beings grow to maturity under an ever-increasing burden of the past, a past that would crush their spirit unless they could to some extent forget it. "Without forgetting," he summed up with aphoristic *éclat*, "it is utterly impossible to live at all."[2] Spurred by Darwin, Nietzsche is arguing for understanding the human past as a problem, and against what he saw as the "modern" tendency to see history only as a benign process of accumulating knowledge. Since our history thrusts itself on our consciousness, there must be a *counterthrust* as well. We must value in human beings the strength to develop uniquely from within, the strength to assimilate and transform the past.

This psychological bias and oppositional cast of mind afforded Nietzsche fresh insight into the way religions maintain their grounding. They promote the simplistic belief that the morality they embrace is absolute, not to be questioned, derived from the authority of "God". And because believers scarcely understand

---

[1] Nietzsche, *Werke in drei Bänden*, v.3, p. 894.
[2] "History in the Service and Disservice of Life," in *Unmodern Observations*, pp. 88-91.

that they are thereby making a false objectification of morality, Nietzsche exposes their thinking with penetrating irony. Under the heading of "God's honesty" he writes: "Would he not be a cruel god if he possessed the truth and could behold mankind miserably tormenting itself over the truth?—But perhaps he is a god of goodness notwithstanding—and merely *could* not express himself more clearly! Did he perhaps lack the intelligence to do so? Or the eloquence?"[3] The mockery becomes increasingly mordant, almost Beckettian, for it is of course *our* lack of honesty and not God's that is in question.

One of the most original aspects of Nietzsche's thinking is the genealogical method he developed to analyze the process by which morality came to be identified with an absolute God and thus universalized. He did not ask whether an idea of God was true or false but how it originated and gained its power. Thus he was not concerned, as atheists were, with refutation. A philosopher should seek to make a "clean sweep."[4] Kant and Schopenhauer had done much to question the metaphysical basis of Christian morality but they hadn't made a clean sweep. After removing support for divinely ordained moral authority in the *Critique of Pure Reason*, Kant turned around in the *Critique of Practical Reason* and in effect re-enthroned this support by way of the categorical imperative. Despite his bold emphasis on the will, Schopenhauer also gave us little insight into the origin of moral ideas because he was mesmerized by the power of aesthetic contemplation to release us from the will's base compulsions and so endorsed the Christian idealization of self-denial, self-sacrifice,

---

3 *Daybreak*, #91.
4 Ibid. #95.

and compassion.⁵ Nietzsche made a similar point about George Eliot and the English in general, who are "rid of the Christian God and are now all the *more* convinced that they have to hold on to Christian morality."⁶

Nietzsche's assault on moral absolutism is often misunderstood as an assault on morality altogether. An important statement such as "There is no such thing as moral phenomena but only moral interpretations of phenomena"⁷ points not at all to moral indifference but to the cogent truth that individuals look at the world from different perspectives and so their moral judgments are necessarily interpretations rather than universal truths. In the preface to *Beyond Good and Evil*, perspective is called "that fundamental condition of all life" because there can be no absolute knowledge of the whole.

This idea has made many readers uneasy and is often condemned as "relativism". But there is an important difference between Nietzschean perspectivism and relativism, ably explained by Robert C. Solomon. Interpretations, he writes, are not abstractly isolated "from any context in which they might be evaluated…. There is *always* such a context, and it is defined in part by the character and circumstances of the person who holds the interpretation." And this, according to Solomon, doesn't lead to a hermeneutic free-for-all because stronger interpretations include more factual evidence, and so are likely to collide with and be modified by other interpretations. Nietzsche's main argument,

---

5   *On the Genealogy of Morals*, Third Essay, #5-6.
6   *Twilight of the Idols*, p. 45.
7   *Beyond Good and Evil*, #108.

he concludes, is directed against the religion-supported belief that there is a moral point of view *in itself*.[8]

In a major essay, "On Truth and Lie in an Extra-Moral Sense," Nietzsche boldly wrote that what we call truths are metaphors that we have forgotten are metaphors and thus "lies" or "errors." But we cannot discard them. The difficult wisdom to be learned is that "truth is the kind of error without which a certain species of life could not live."[9] Fields of knowledge that generate warmer emotions, like religion and the arts, are at greater risk here, but science is not exempt, as shown by its tendency to speak of the laws and purposes of nature, implying a supreme, metaphysical standard. Nietzsche wanted us to understand that, while Darwin's science had unsettled religion, it could not do the work of religion. Yet religion, more than other discourses, tended to dogmatize about morality, thus making "atheism" a particularly liberating idea. For this philosopher, atheism meant in general the freedom to question everything. "The man of faith, the 'believer' of every sort is necessarily a dependent man,"[10] but for the creative man intellectual dependence is hardly tolerable. As Zarathustra put it, "what could one create if gods existed."[11] Indeed," a complete and definitive victory of atheism might deliver mankind altogether from its feeling of indebtedness: and thus constitute "a second innocence."[12]

"Definitive victory" expresses Nietzsche's philosophic aim in its utopian aspect, evoking the possibility of dissolving current

---

8   Solomon, "Nietzsche ad hominem," pp. 198-201.
9   *The Will to Power*, p. 493.
10 *Twilight of the Idols*, p. 172.
11 *Thus Spake Zarathustra*, p. 87.
12 *On the Genealogy of Morals*, Second Essay, #20.

values. But such dissolution poses also the prospect of "weightlessness," "the void," "nihilism." In a utopian mood, Nietzsche like Zarathustra pictures "the higher man" as a free-floating self-creator, cheerful and elevated at once. In *The Gay Science* (#343) such a figure welcomes the bracing prospect of an "open sea" and a "new dawn" wherein "all weight is to be determined anew." Nihilism was a potentially creative matrix, allowing for a rethinking of fundamentals. *The Will to Power* offers this definition of that arresting word: "*That the highest values devaluate themselves* [because] 'why' finds no answer."[13] In his multi-volume study of his predecessor Heidegger singles out this passage to demonstrate that Nietzsche looks at nihilism as a spur to a "creative countermove."[14]

Given this much contextualization of the God question in Nietzsche's philosophy, let us turn to the notorious cry "God is dead" in the parable of the madman from *The Gay Science* (#125).

Because the Christian God is a cultural rather than supernatural phenomenon, to say that he is dead is to suggest that certain theistic ideas (God the Father, the Judge, the Redeemer of men) have lost their significance in the modern age. But Nietzsche hardly wished to live in a morally insignificant age and was therefore concerned that others, unprepared for the challenge to replace God out of their own self-making were belittling the event's importance. The parable is full of ironic implications, and I will spell out three of them here.

---

13 *Will to Power*, p. 9.
14 Heidegger, *Nietzsche*, p. 26. Karl Jaspers said much the same thing: "Nietzsche saw in atheism not simply a loss but rather the greatest opportunity." Quoted by Walter Kaufmann, *Existentialism*, p. 194 See also Kaufmann, *Nietzsche*,. p. 422.

Those hearing the madman who did not believe in God laugh at his cry as if he were raving. They think they have discarded faith based in supernaturalism but are retaining it through their faith in the moral coherence of the world. They fear that the loss of such coherence would "wipe away the entire horizon" and thereby induce a sense of "straying...through an infinite nothing." To say that god is dead, writes Richard Rorty, is to say that human beings "serve no higher purposes,"[15] but these listeners are not prepared to live in so undefined a world.

The second implication has three aspects. The parable is given to us by a madman because, first, only a madman can break the grip of custom and so prepare the way for a new understanding; second, someone possessed of the knowledge that God is dead is maddened by it; and third, being "mad" or clowning is a way of recognizing the fact that others are not ready for this knowledge. It takes time to discard the old religion altogether. The madman is an anti-Christ or even a new Christ, knowing that for the tidings he brings "my time is not yet."

A third implication of the parable worth clarifying here is that it presents ideas as events. It says that "we ourselves" have already done the murderous deed yet also that "the event is on the way." Although it is illogical to talk about an event as both behind and before us, it makes sense if one is talking about the movement of ideas, especially about the unconscious or underlying tendency in such movement. When people at last understand their condition, they will have need of a new bible, like *Thus Spake Zarathustra* about to be written. For the need to will something outlives the death of God. Man, we are told at the end of *A Gene-*

---

15 Rorty, p. 120.

alogy of Morals, "would rather will nothingness than not will at all."

In fact what has unsettled Nietzsche's readers more than his atheism (which, as the parable implies, is anything but direct), is the appearance in his work of moral relativism, a subject that requires further clarification. It would seem to make little sense to call Nietzsche a moral relativist since his work is full of strong assertion that, for all their ironies, are evidently asking to be taken seriously. But if "convictions are prisons" (as he puts it in *Ecce Homo*), what about his own convictions? Alexander Nehamas resolves the paradox by explaining that, while Nietzsche knows that his truths are views, he knows also that for him they are truths. The implied model here is the literary text, about which a sophisticated interpreter would say neither that one view is absolute nor that it is no better (or worse) than any other, for one view can be stronger or weaker than another. To understand "this most literary of philosophers," Nehamas writes, "we must see that his "aestheticism is the other side of his perspectivism." And he demonstrates skillfully how Nietzsche's variety of styles supports this idea, for these styles show us perspectives without weakening the demonstration by *telling* us that they are perspectives.[16]

Nehamas candidly adds, "It is hard to avoid the suspicion that Nietzsche had little of positive value to say." *The Will to Power* talks of meaninglessness as a "transitional stage," but is vague about a goal. Transition to what? Nonetheless, the positive *tone* in his work is unmistakable. Nietzsche idealized as energetically as he questioned. He unstintingly admired the nobility of ancient Greek culture; found exemplary status in Wagner and Schopen-

---

16 Nehamas, *Nietzsche: Life as Literature,* pp. 98, 8.

hauer before his break with the one and disagreements with the other; never ceased to admire the Olympian Goethe, whom he called Dionysian after the word acquired new resonance for him; and about Emerson's work, cherished from youth, he wrote "I have never in a book felt myself so much at home....I dare not praise it, it is so close to me."[17] Moreover, words like "joy," "life-enhancing," "health," and "strength" intensify his rhetoric and are lexically characteristic. Repudiation of God was for him hardly a negative but the necessary prelude to the bracing and open-ended work of self-creation. I will therefore round out my picture of Nietzsche as "meta-theist" by commenting on three of his notable slogans—*Übermensch*, Will to Power, and Eternal Return. Each clarifies his effort to think beyond religion without quite embracing a new religion.

Nietzsche liked to distinguish "noble" and "base" types of human being and culture. The one is "complete, wholly successful, happy, powerful, triumphant"; the other is "more good-natured, cleverer, more comfortable, more mediocre...more Christian."[18] But the positive words do not quite describe the *Übermensch*, for in *Zarathustra* (where the slogan is most fully articulated) the most distinct attribute of the "overman" is an endless becoming and strenuous self-overcoming. The overman thrives on opposition, digests pain, absorbs suffering. It was Nietzsche who more than anyone else taught us (in *The Birth of Tragedy*) that the complete and successful art of ancient Greece was infused by a strong Dionysian element—"how much did this people have to suffer to be able to become so beautiful!" The overman, then, is best seen as a prophetic figure, not a person who has already overcome his

---

17 Quoted by George Stack, *Nietzsche and Emerson*, p. 44.
18 *Genealogy of Morals*, First Essay #12.

all-too-human self but one who is ever in the process of doing so. The English translation closest in spirit to this idea, though awkward, is "the beyond man," used by George Stack in his book on Nietzsche and Emerson. The single quality that best defines the type is exuberance. He is potential man, both anti-Christ and anti-nihilist, who might arise at some future time.

The Will to Power is a phrase that lends itself to misunderstanding (made more complicated by the political bias of Nietzsche's sister, who edited his unpublished manuscripts) but it is too important to be ignored. This concept, we can see, is basically psychological rather than political. Like Schopenhauer's *Wille*, which it seeks to revise, it denotes instinctual energy but an energy that can become moral and intellectual, and is not merely energy as a biological endowment. To link it with self-preservation as Schopenhauer does or with the struggle for existence as Darwin does implies that the will is merely natural rather than, also, a will strong enough to rise *above nature.* He wants the brutal or violent aspect of passion to be restrained not simply by a censoring faculty but by the stronger passion of self-overcoming, a process of sublimation that anticipates Freud. For him, as Walter Kaufmann puts it, "the highest degree of power consists of self-mastery,"[19] which is something different from controlling one's passions or even from quieting them. A good way to understand what it means for him is to notice how it might be applied in a theory of aesthetic response. For Kant and Schopenhauer art quiets the will whereas for Nietzsche (as for Stendhal) art stimulates the will.

The Eternal Return, introduced in *The Gay Science* and developed in *Zarathustra* and thereafter, is still more complex and in

---

19 Kaufmann, *Nietzsche: Philosopher, Psychologist, Antichrist*, p. 252.

truth not quite coherent. It is perhaps best explicated by detouring through Nietzsche's analysis of the "ascetic ideal".

The story of the Christian conscience goes something like this. Once upon a time there were the noble Greeks, whose legacy, alas, was pushed aside by ignoble Christianity and its later complement, democracy. The gods of their polytheistic religion did not judge or pity human beings, and so kept bad conscience at a distance. Thus the Greeks were beyond *ressentiment*, the mainspring of "the slave rebellion in morals" initiated by Judeo-Christianity. In Epicurus pain was a source of strength whereas for Christians it became a source of fear.

Like others after him who have speculated on the decline of the West, Nietzsche does not know exactly whom to blame for this degradation. Perhaps the rabble got the upper hand and led us into Christianity. Perhaps the trouble began with the Salvationist morality taught by Jesus and Paul, for sometimes Nietzsche contrasts the naïve consciousness of power and self-delight in the Old Testament with the fussier, more sectarian spirit of the New. But he also thought of the whole Bible as a miserable affair among Jews, as in *The Gay Science*, #135: "Sin as it is experienced wherever Christianity now holds sway or has held sway is a Jewish feeling and a Jewish invention." "The Jew" (i.e. Jesus, although *The Anti-Christ* puts the onus on Paul) was the baleful originator, teaching goodness and pity rather than power, and creating a sinful conscience. Nietzsche was not anti-Semitic in the sense that the Wagners were. In one strong passage (*Human, All Too Human* [#475]) he even shows himself to be an anti-anti-Semite. But he did exploit an anti-Semitic vocabulary in his attacks on Christianity. In effect he blamed Christianity on the Jews. His view is curiously similar to that of Freud, who in *Moses and*

Monotheism sought to explain the anti-Semitism exploding around him as revenge against Christianity for the curbing of instinctual freedom.

Nietzsche is working with a very broad brush here, but the psychological nub of his argument is sharp-edged. As the old insouciant freedom of the instincts was restricted and disciplined by new doctrines of moral accountability, people began to blame themselves for their frustration and suffering. They began to feel sin and guilt, which turned into torment the kind of suffering that an Epicurus had robustly absorbed. That is, suffering led to more suffering by way of conscience, an analysis not very different from Freud's of the origin of the superego. A god of love and pity intensely close to us reinforced this misery. Pity ("self-pity's kin" when there is a "too too human god," according to Wallace Stevens in "Esthétique du Mal") thus weds us to "the ascetic ideal." Only a strong spirit like Zarathustra can cry out, "Pity is obtrusive [and] offends our sense of shame." But modern democracy is the heir of Christianity and has taken over this enervating morality of goodness.

Nietzsche's personal stake in this attack on Christianity is somewhat puzzling, and it is fair to interrogate it because *Beyond Good and Evil* begins by advising us to consider what is personally at stake in any philosopher's thought. There is little evidence of lasting grievance directed at his Lutheran background. References to his father, who died when Nietzsche was not yet five years old, are friendly, and, although he may have unconsciously transferred some resentment concerning his father's early death to that father's religion, he seems to have had no quarrel with practicing Christians (like his loyal friend, Franz Overbeck) or with the Church itself, from which he broke for reasons quite understandable in terms of the needs of a highly original mind for intellectual independence. But the principal fact about Nietzsche's productive years, along with his extraordinary creativity, was the suffering he endured as a result of persistent illness and the restrictions it imposed. His was largely an ascetic life.

This suffering must have seemed meaningless and arbitrary until he discovered a way to explain it. Christian morality tended to blame the sufferer, teaching him to internalize blame as a sense of sin. This teaching Nietzsche bravely repudiated, calling it the theology of a "hangman-god." But he did eventually find the meaning of his life in pain itself. Zarathustra pointedly contrasts "My hangman-god" to "My unknown god! My *pain!* My last—happiness!" Nietzsche must have sensed that the ascetic ideal was not so different from his own, for he now spoke of it as an attempt to wrest meaning from life, seeing that it could provide an escape from nihilism. Thus (as the Third Essay of *Genealogy of Morals* begins and ends) "man would rather will *nothingness* than not will at all." Which brings us back to the Eternal Return.

This strange doctrine holds that everything that happens has already happened and will be exactly repeated ad infinitum. It apparently makes a cosmological claim, but critics have not been impressed by this, perhaps sensing that the psychological equivalent ("nothing in my life could have been otherwise") sounds more like what is really meant. Nietzsche imagined the Eternal Return, despite or because of the fact that it first induced nausea in him, as "the highest affirmation attainable." *Ecce Homo* expands on this idea: "My formula for greatness in a human being is *amor fati*, that one wants nothing to be other than it is, not in the future, not in the past, not in all eternity." The challenge, then, was not simply to endure but to love fate, not simply to learn how to accept oneself but "how to become what one is," the subtitle of *Ecce Homo*. W. B. Yeats, in his poem "The Gyres," caught the spirit of the Latin phrase *amor fati* in his free translation, "tragic joy," a phrasing that is particularly suggestive because it enables us to link Nietzsche last book with his first, self-making with tragedy.

In 1872 Nietzsche had associated Dionysus with pain and suffering that turned into joy by way of aesthetic experience: "it is only in aesthetic terms that the world is eternally justified." But in 1886, writing an "Attempt at a Self-Criticism" prefacing the reissued *Birth of Tragedy*, he draws back from this formulation, telling us that the earlier statement "made the world at every moment the *attained* salvation of God."[20]

In 1872 Nietzsche wanted to aestheticize the universe and thus thought of the artist as an aspect of God: "the genius in the act of creation merges with the primal architect of the cosmos." But in 1886 he wanted to attempt the more difficult task of aestheticizing himself. Thus divinity would become an aspect of artistic genius rather than the other way around. Dionysus now is not just the energy to be transformed into beauty but another name for the artist, which is to say for himself. In 1872 he had agreed with Schopenhauer that tragedy captured the paradox of existence. But in his later work he saw himself as that tragedy, transforming the pain of existence into ultimate meaning. He would become his own Redeemer. In the essay "We Classicists" he had written: "My religion, if I must use a word of that sort, lies in the task of producing the genius.... Religion is *love beyond our-*

---

20 *The Birth of Tragedy*, p. 144.

selves. The work of art is *the perfect image of such self-transcending love.*"[21]

There could never be a community of Nietzcheans, a religious movement as we ordinarily understand that phrase. In calling himself the Antichrist or implying, when he used the name Dionysus that he was a type of Christ, in titling the autobiographical *Ecce Homo* with an allusion to Christ, Nietzsche must have known that he was identifying himself finally with Christianity. But he also knew he could never redeem anyone but himself, that his truest disciples, like Zarathustra's, would not follow him but would find their own way.

Nehamas wryly called Nietzsche "the first of the last of the metaphysicians." One thinks of various twentieth-century figures influenced by him who have tried to be last of the last. There is Heidegger, trying to elude what Derrida would call a metaphysics of presence by reconfiguring the concept of being. There is Foucault, whose own genealogical method owes much to Nietzsche, teaching the diffusion of authorial agency. And of course there is Derrida, trying through deconstruction to explain the master's emphasis on perpetual change in terms of endlessly deferred meaning. Perhaps there will never be a last metaphysician since one's presuppositions about the ulterior relations of ideas have a way of being exposed by later philosophy. But Nietzsche certainly pointed the way. He liked to use a plural pronoun in speaking of the exemplary person—we philosophers, we opposite men, we modern men, we free spirits, our cheerfulness." This is a *dream* of community since such a person is always single and always changing. In the last analysis, Nietzsche's idealizations are always "beyond," beyond definitive moral or theological

---

21 *Unmodern Observations*, p. 350.

formulation. His doctrine of man's ever-changing potential for self-realization leads *toward* some supreme idealization but can never settle on one. His brand of antitheism might best be described as metatheism.

Mark Twain's Countertheology

Samuel Clemens (better known as Mark Twain) was too enraged by the deity he knew—the trainer of his "Presbyterian conscience," as he freely admitted early in his *Autobiography*[1]—to speculate coolly on his existence. God had to be exposed or opposed, not with philosophic argument but with language tart and vivid enough to drive home his cruelty, injustice and absurdity.

The "damned human race" was theologically damned because God determined both man's character and his behavior. But the attack on God can be made as well through *man* and *his* damnable ways. In practice, an indictment of one usually slides into an indictment of the other:

> [The Bible] begins with an inexcusable treachery, and that is the keynote of the entire Biography. [Ignorant Adam could not have been expected to understand the prohibition, yet] his posterity individual by individual, has been unceasingly hunted and harried with afflictions in punishment of the juvenile misdemeanor, which is grandiloquently called Adam's sin. And during all that vast lapse of time, there has been no lack of rabbins and popes and bishops and priests and parsons and lay slaves eager to ap-

---

1   Neider (ed.) *Autobiography of Mark Twain*, p. 44.

plaud this infamy, maintain the unassailable justice and righteousness of it, and praise.[2]

[God] has almost bankrupted his native ingenuities in inventing pains and miseries and humiliations and heartbreaks wherewith to embitter the brief lives of Adam's descendants....Then...the gifted Christian blandly calls him Our Father!...He equips the Creator with every trait that goes to the making of a fiend, and then arrives at the conclusion that a fiend and a father are the same thing![3]

Twain understands well enough that deities are man-made. But, unlike Feuerbach and Nietzsche, he chooses to blur rather than sharpen the distinction between theology and psychology, and thus to insist on the image of an anthropomorphic divine fiend, never mind the lack of logical finesse. No wonder his minister friend Joseph Twichell complained that he was "too orthodox in the Doctrine of Total Human Depravity."[4]

From the 1870s, Twain's theological orientation was influenced also by his reading of Paine's deistic *The Age of Reason* and by his exposure to nineteenth-century scientific thinking about time and space, disease, and the Bible. Some of his critics have suggested that these influences sophisticated his theology, but this isn't exactly the case. He seized on the critique of the Bible that he found in Paine and the Higher Criticism to intensify his quarrel with the Bible's God rather than to ease his need to mount it. He did not wish to seek a compromise between "primitive" and "abstract" theologies because his narrative art required for its ironic effects their collision and clash.

---

2 Baetzhold and McCullough (eds.), *Bible According to Mark Twain*, pp. 319-20.
3 Ibid., pp., 228-239.
4 Quoted in Andrews, *Nook Farm*, chapter 2.

Thus a theology of general Providence, featuring a Creator working by remote, impersonal law, did not replace the old hated theology of special Providence with its emphasis on a caring and loving Father because the artist saw the advantage of having them play against and across one another. When a deistic God of immutable law is invoked, this soon turns into the old anthropomorphic fiend. A passage that begins, "Let us now consider the real God, the genuine God... whose remotenesses are visited by comets only," turns after a page or two into this: "We know that the real God... made all the creatures, from the microbe and the brontosaur down to the man and the monkey, and that He knew what would happen to each and every one of them from the beginning of time to the end of it. In the case of each creature, big or little, He made it an unchanging law that that creature should suffer wanton and unnecessary pains and miseries every day of its life."[5] The deist God, then, is fodder for irony. At times even the language of deism is parodied, as in *Letters from the Earth*, where God is said to create now a predator and now a victim, each in turn declared blameless because it is obeying "a law of nature"– and "the law of nature is the Law of God."[6]

The diatribe "What Is Man?" attempts to combine an updated determinism with the old fundamentalism rather than to exploit the incongruity between them, and loses much of its effectiveness thereby. Humor was essential to Twain's art. In an important letter of 1865 to his brother Orion, the young writer understood he had "a calling to literature of a low order," which, he admitted, is "nothing to be proud of" but "my strongest suit."[7] He was right

---

5 Neider (ed.), "Mark Twain's 'Reflections on Religion,'" pp. 343-46.
6 DeVoto (ed.), *Letters from the Earth*, p. 5.
7 Quoted in Brodwin, "Theology of Mark Twain," p. 222.

about this, yet right also when he wrote in the *Autobiography*: "I have always preached....if the humor came of its own accord and uninvited, I have allowed it a place in my sermon."[8] It is the varying combinations of preaching and humor that define his narrative art and account for its characteristics. Twain's brand of antitheism is therefore much less dogmatic than, say, that of Charles Bradlaugh, who also wrote screeds against the Bible and Christian doctrine but who piled up his indictment in a hard analytic style that, while forceful, had no real bite. Mark Twain's satirical humor is complicit with his own conflicting emotions, with his own sense of human unworthiness as well as his own strength, and hence more telling in its effect on us. Bradlaugh is fighting a political battle only while Mark Twain is also wrestling with something in himself, and result is not mere "rhetoric" but "art."

What is he preaching? A pretty good short answer is "Man's cruel and unjust banishment from Eden." It was offered by Stanley Brodwin, who in a series of essays developed the fruitful idea of Mark Twain's "countertheology."[9] Its core is a revisionary myth of the biblical Adam, an Everyman who is innocent because before the Fall he had no Moral Sense and so could not sin, yet was punished *with* a Moral Sense prompting him to exalt himself as the "delight" of the very God that torments his conscience. Such a formulation illuminates the oeuvre, not only the later fables, because Twain's early and middle fictions feature a gradually more desperate Adam figure who finally turns into an irreverent and articulate exposer and opposer of God called "Satan."

---

8 Neider (ed.), *Autobiography of Mark Twain*, p. 298.

9 Brodwin developed the concept of Twain's "countertheology" in "Theology of Mark Twain: Banished Adam and the Bible" (1976) and extended it in "Mark Twain in the Pulpit: The Theological Comedy of *Huckleberry Finn*" (1985) and "Theology of Mark Twain" in *Cambridge Companion* (1988).

Brodwin identifies the key questions raised by his revisionary myth under three headings: Providence, Lies, and Moral Reform. Providence (the special Providence of the Calvinist tradition rather than the general Providence of the deists) is above all treacherous because it offers salvation and personal love—immense "sarcasms" in view of God's cruelties. By "Lies" Brodwin understands Twain to mean the timidity and conceit that motivate man to exalt this God and commit horrendous cruelties in His name. Since Providence and Lies—the indictment of God and of Man—are complementary topics, Moral Reform seems to make an odd third item in the group, but it is in fact crucial. Twain's brand of Protestantism promoted entrepreneurial initiative, and this must have been augmented by the nineteenth-century American faith in energy, progress, and prosperity that shaped the writer even as he deplored its excesses. His earlier Adamic figures seek to evade reform because they distrust "sivilization": his later ones (Hank Morgan, Roxana, Joan of Arc) must try to alter history and must fail. The impossibility of reform is central to his vision of man, but we may be puzzled by the bitterness of this conviction unless we see it as the disillusioned result of a thirst *for* reform.

The biblical Adam was a favorite image from early on, and acquired even more significance as the narrative art turned gradually away from realism toward fable. As early as 1853 (at the age of seventeen) Twain styled himself "a son of Adam" in a squib for his brother's *Hannibal Journal,* and the personal identification remained. In a letter of 1887, replying to an old friend's evocation of childhood days, he said he felt like "a banished Adam" revisiting a half-forgotten Paradise."[10] During the 1870s, after some dabbling with Noah and Methuselah stories, he wrote "Adam's

---

10 Quoted in Brodwin, "Theology of Mark Twain," p. 167.

Expulsion," the first of many attempts featuring Adam as the chief character of a sketch. Most of these sketches were composed between 1893 and 1905, and carried such titles as "Adam's Diary," "Eve's Diary," "Adam's Soliloquy," "Papers of the Adam Family," and "That Day in Eden" (in which the pathos of the First Family's situation is expressed by Satan—not to mention various references to Adam in the novels and travel books, in Pudd'nhead Wilson's "Calendar," and in Satan-centered pieces like "Letters from the Earth." Inventing material centered on Adam allowed for whimsical humor by way of anachronisms, but the basic idea of God's injustice is not lost sight of. The best strokes are the sardonic ones. Wilson notes in his "Calendar": "Adam was but human—that explains it all. He did not want the apple for the apple's sake, he wanted it only because it was forbidden. The mistake was in not forbidding the serpent; then he would have eaten the serpent." Another is Satan's wry comment on mankind's first parents: "Adam and Eve think ill of death—they will change their mind."[11]

The development of the Adamic figure in Twain's art reaches one climax in *Huckleberry Finn*. The narrators of *Innocents Abroad* and *Roughing It* alternate uncertainly between the joy of fresh discovery and dismay at what is discovered. But, after exposing corruptions of the Reconstructionist era in *The Gilded Age*, Twain developed—in *Tom Sawyer*, *Life on the Mississippi*, and especially *Huckleberry Finn*—a more complex tension between a natural man and the fallen world in which that figure must live. Tom and Huck live in a world of harrying prohibitions and dishonest theology but they are not quite *of* that world; they preserve their unfallen condition "down here below" (to use Huck's own phrase),

---

11 See "Eve's Diary," in DeVoto (ed.), *The Bible According to Mark Twain*, p. 70.

by instinctive irreverence, disguise, cunning evasion, and even by lies against lies. It is not easy for them to preserve their freedom from civilized values because these values have to some extent been internalized. A prime example is Huck's decision to lie, in spite of conscience, concerning Jim. He has sufficient natural wisdom to resist the crippling Moral Sense, and, since he is going to hell anyway, has no need to reform. He and Jim may be called pre-Christian or pagan, as in their charming speculation on whether the stars just happened or were made by the moon. That the Adamic is not a simple idea is made clear by the fact that vicious Pap represents another version of it. He is the natural man as unregenerate and filthy. "Like Adam," comments Huck disgustedly, "he was all mud." But Pap has all the credentials: he has no use for Providence, never lies to himself (however repellent his opinions), and will never reform. After discovering how far Pap has exploited his hospitality and benevolent resolve "to make a man of him," "the new judge...felt kind of sore. He said he reckoned a body could reform the old man with a shotgun, maybe, but he didn't know no other way."[12]

Although there is no false romance in the Mississippi River trilogy, in the largest efforts of the following decade—*A Connecticut Yankee in King Arthur's Court, Pudd'nhead Wilson,* and *Joan of Arc*—Twain seems to hurl himself against romance itself as if to assert that it is no longer enough for civilization to be merely resisted by an Adamic consciousness: it must also be reformed. None of these books is very successful (although *Pudd'nhead Wilson* is quite readable), but all are interestingly conflicted in conception. Twain is both impatient with societies that fear to re-

---

12 While working on this novel, Twain wrote a piece called "Recent Crime in Connecticut" (1876) that exposes the "natural man" as a killer.

form and aware that any society (including his own) will resist reform. They are worth brief comment because they help to account for the turn in the last decades to a fabling mode of narrative art in which a stubbornly oppressive theology is countered by original deployments of Adam and Satan.

In the burlesque plot of *Connecticut Yankee*, Hank Morgan is thrown magically back into the world of medieval chivalry and attempts, as the ever resourceful "Boss," to blow it all up, replacing it entirely with democracy, freedom from religion, and all the boons of nineteenth-century progress. He goes very far before being stopped by a Church Interdict and Merlin's accompanying machinations, but perhaps he is stopped even more by losing confidence in his right the mount the total violence required to root out the foundations of a cowardly society. Twain wrote in *Life on the Mississippi* that the Civil War was started by the South's love of Sir Walter Scott, and certainly the false romance of chivalry is one of his targets in this book, but that hardly explains the earnestness and thoroughness of Hank's enterprise, or its failure. Brodwin asks the right question about the author's motives: "Why go into the past to form a democratic Utopia—and then destroy it—if that Utopia exists, however imperfectly, in the present?"[13] What stops the Boss is not made altogether clear in this novel "at war with itself," in Bernard DeVoto's words,[14] but the author seems to have sensed the problem because, as James D. Williams observed, his revisions work in the direction of making Hank gradually less of an ignoramus, more sophisticated and

---

13 Brodwin, "Wandering Between Two Gods", *Studies in the Literary Imagination*, pp.57-82.
14 DeVoto," in Bloom (ed.), *Mark Twain: Modern Critical Views*, 26.

aware.[15] The philosopher Alfred North Whitehead reflected on the general problem raised by this kind of experiment. "It may be impossible," he wrote, "to conceive a reorganization of society adequate for the removal of some admitted evil without destroying the social organization of the civilization which depends on it."[16] Twain himself must have realized that radical reform was as impossible in the sixth century as in the nineteenth. And if the hope of progress must then be compromised, what else can an author do finally with Hank Morgan than to bring him back to the present, let him give his testimony to M. T., and die?

A somewhat similar dialectic of despair underlies *Pudd'nhead Wilson*. The slave Roxana seeks to reform the manifest injustice of the treatment of blacks in her society by switching babies in the cradle and allowing her "Tom" to live as a white man. But she must fail because she cannot reform the total structure of injustice, which derives not exactly from being black but from being black in a society ruled by whites, from living in a society built upon the myth that blacks are different. Justice (after a fashion) is served when in a grand courtroom finale Wilson cleverly proves Tom guilty of a crime. Tom would be sent to prison if he were white but is spared that fate because, as a black slave, he is a valuable and exploitable piece of property. The "justice" of that outcome (real justice being impossible within a racist society) is reported by the narrator with a smartly ironic flourish:

> Everybody granted that if Tom were white and free it would be unquestionably right to punish him—it would be no loss to any-

---

15 Williams, in *American Literature*, v. 36, pp. 288-297.
16 Whitehead, *Adventures in Ideas*, p. 24.

body, but to shut up a valuable slave for life—that was another matter.

As soon as the Governor understood the case, he pardoned Tom at once, and the creditors sold him down the river.

Wilson's role in the book seems odd because he is hardly involved in the action until the end, but, largely through his "Calendar" (the reputed source of the chapter-epigraphs), he serves as sardonic commentator of the American society he knows. His final entry sums it up: "It was wonderful to find America, but it would have been more wonderful to miss it."

The humorless, hagiographic Joan of Arc book is less complex but no less desperate. Twain develops from the records the noblest human image he can put into words and pits it against the combined Church and State, with a foregone conclusion. We read at one point about "God's good gift of laughter," but this is nowhere in evidence, and it appears that Twain himself was losing faith in its efficacy. In one of *The Mysterious Stranger* manuscripts written about the same time, Satan teaches that "nothing can stand" against "the assault of laughter"—and the assault he has in mind is directed against Catholic and Presbyterian orthodoxy. But the same passage adds dismayingly that the human race lacks the sense and courage to "ever use it at all."[17]

History, ransacked by Twain, yielded a litany of barbarities, nor was any nation exempt. The St. Bartholomew Day massacre in sixteenth-century France was "unquestionably the finest thing of its kind ever devised."[18] The satirist's pained conscience did, however, go out to the underdog—to the Negro because of

---

17 Gibson (ed.), *Mark Twain's Mysterious Stranger Manuscripts*, p. 166.
18 DeVoto (ed.), *Letters from the Earth*, p. 183.

lynchings and the Jew because of pogroms and certainly to non-human animals whom in our conceit we feel superior. Words like "brutal" and "bestial" describing human behavior always elicit an ironic response from the satirist, who delights in showing that "inhuman" behavior is simply the most characteristically "human" behavior of all. One piece about the so-called "highest animal" is called "The Lowest Animal."

From the mid-1890s until his death in 1910 the root idea of Mark Twain's various and often unfinished literary ventures is that both God and Man are insane. What then is left for the moral humorist to do? He chose to spin off the Adamic myth by building up the figure of Satan, an unfallen but knowing Adam who could comment on this insanity with some detachment, hence with irony as well as preacherly denunciation.

The *Autobiography* tells us that its author had "always felt friendly toward Satan."[19] In the late work, remarks to this effect develop into sketches (with titles like "Satan's Diary," "Sold to Satan," "Letters to Satan," "A Humane Word from Satan") or are worked up into longer narratives like *Letters from the Earth* and *The Mysterious Stranger*. Moreover, several stories that rather boldly venture into preternatural territory—"The Man that Corrupted Hadleyburg," "Captain Stormfield's Visit to Heaven" (especially the latter half of it, known as Sandy's narrative), "The Great Dark"—are clearly linked to the Satan figure without mentioning him.[20] As William M. Gibson put it, "the Satanic stranger, who visits the earth and pities and judges men, dominated his

---

19 Neider (ed.), *Autobiography of Mark Twain*, p. 18,
20 Neider (ed.), *Complete Short Stories of Mark Twain*, pp. 419-814.

imagination and guided his pen in those years, trailing dozens of lesser characters in his angelic wake."[21]

In *Letters from the Earth* Satan is imagined as reporting back home to St. Michael and St. Gabriel on how the Human Race experiment is coming along. He finds the earth to be a strange, appalling place: "The people are all insane, the other animals are all insane, the earth is insane, nature itself is insane." Yet "Man is a marvelous curiosity." Several features of Man seem to him especially curious. Man's constant compliments to God are unconscious "sarcasms...uttered without a smile." His Heaven is dishonest, containing nothing he really values like sexual intercourse. His God does indeed have his eye on the poor since "nine-tenths of hid disease-inventions" are bestowed on them. And his God's New Testament, which brought Hell, is even worse than the Old, which brought Life and Death, for "the Deity perceived that death was a mistake, a mistake in that it was insufficient, insufficient in that, while it was an admirable agent for the inflicting of misery on the survivor, it allowed the dead person himself to escape from all further persecution in the blessed refuge of the grave." Satan has much more to say on the malice of God, for his pen was indeed "warmed in hell," as Twain told his friend William Dean Howells he wished his own to be.[22]

The manuscripts of *The Mysterious Stranger* yield no definitive single version, but there are important constants. In all of them "Satan" is a figure from another world who imparts dark truth to an adolescent boy. He is called "Philip Traum" in one of the fullest

---

21 Gibson, "Introduction," *Mark Twain's Mysterious Stranger Manuscripts*, p.19. Most of the narrative is reprinted in DeVoto (ed), *Complete Short Stories of Mark Twain*, pp. 721-814,
22 Quoted by DeVoto, in Bloom, ed. Mark Twain: *Modern Critical Views*, p. 15.

manuscripts, and does in fact become a sort of "Superintendent of Dreams" (the name given a satanic figure in another long story, "The Great Dark") as he demonstrates his dark magic to the boy, who serves as narrator and bewildered interpreter. Satan plays various roles in relation to the people in the boy's world—pedagogue, exuberant magician, scornful punisher, pitying consoler—roles that seem inconsistent but allow for different ironic strategies by which the free-wheeling author can express his total contempt for the Human Race and its vaunted Moral Sense. Of course the God who created Man is understood to be ultimately at fault, but Twain never hesitates to blame Man, the worshiper of this God, at the same time.

With this last major effort, however, the author's extreme misanthropy does perhaps drive him into a narrative corner. Unwilling to compromise his indictment, Twain reaches in this tale for the only mitigation he can imagine, which is to have the boy discover under Satan's tutelage that the whole show has been nothing but an unreal dream. But, lest that device come across as itself a compromise, he takes one further (and perhaps narratricdal) step, letting the boy-narrator learn from Satan that even he, the dreamer, is not real. "There is no God, no universe, no human race, no earthly life, no heaven, no hell. It is all a Dream, a grotesque and foolish dream. Nothing exists but You. And you are but a *Thought*—a vagrant Thought, a useless Thought, a homeless Thought, wandering forlorn among the empty eternities!" "He vanished," concludes the narrator, "and left me appalled; for I knew, and realized that all he had said was true."[23] This famous ending was meant by its author to be consoling, for, shortly after his wife's death, he wrote to Twichell that such an

---

23 DeVoto (ed.), *Stories*, p. 714.

idea "reconciles everything, makes everything lucid and understandable."[24] But Satan's "truth" in effect marks the author's retreat from his satire as it dissolves around him, and greatly weakens the force of adding that the boy is "appalled."

"The Mysterious Stranger" demonstrates the limit of Mark Twain's countertheology. Here the mythmaker declares plainly enough, through an exemplary speaker, "there is no God." Yet this idea is inseparable from another: "there is no world." Not unlike Captain Ahab and Moby Dick, the hater and the object of his hatred end up bound together in doom. As Howells early on told his friend, you have "remained a creature of the Presbyterian God who did make you."[25]

---

24 Quoted by Gibson, Introduction to Twain's *Mysterious Stranger Manuscripts*, p. 30.
25 Quoted by Brodwin in *Cambridge Companion to Mark Twain*, p. 242.

The Poetry of Doubt:
Thomas Hardy's Antitheism

Hardy was not a systematic thinker but a poet and novelist imaginatively filtering ideas that attracted him to express a particular experience and world view. This is a point he made repeatedly, as if to correct readers who were looking for a "philosophy." In one prefatory essay, he describes his writings as "unadjusted impressions" having "little cohesion"; in another he asserted that "Positive views on the Whence and the Wherefore of things have never been advanced by this pen as a consistent philosophy"; and in yet another he advised that "no harmonious philosophy is attempted in these pages—or in any bygone pages of mine."[1] It is fitting to ask, then, to what earlier poetic myths his own are most deeply indebted, and a good answer might be Shelley's eros that must fail of its own excess, Swinburne's pagan subversion of Christianity, and the Bible's Yahweh, a presence neither quite personal nor quite transcendent, as God later became in Christian theology, but whose will is incommensurate with that of his people. Hardy called this ultra-human presence Immanent Will,

---

1 "Prefatory Note" in Gibson, ed, *Complete Poems*, p. 85; "General Preface" in Seymour-Smith, ed., *Mayor of Casterbridge*, p. 417; "Introductory Note" in Gibson, ed. *Complete Poems*, p. 834.

Law, Cause, Unconsciousness, and other quasi-anthropomorphic names, adjusting his idea of God to the deterministic notions that he derived both from the irrationalism of Schopenhauer and the rationalism of Darwin.

During the formative period of his development, in the 1860s and 70s, his thinking was also influenced by such systematic thinkers as Huxley, Spencer, Mill, Comte, and Stephen. And we can better understand his particular response to the God question if we consider how his "doubt" differs from theirs. His theme of bafflement in the face of a cosmic will was a product of temperament whereas their principled doubt was the product of logical reasoning. Hardy wrote frankly from his emotions—a gamut of emotions ranging from nostalgia to bitterness. Divine Will in his work confronts man through personifications expressing largely negative but humanly recognizable attitudes—hostility, indifference, uncertainty, sardonic amusement—which elicit a recognizably human response. He merely toyed with conceptual labels, claiming at one point to be "a harmless agnostic" mistaken for a "clamorous atheist."[2]

Dictated to his second wife by Hardy himself, *The Life of Thomas Hardy* quotes him as saying, "I have been looking for God 50 years, and I think that if he had existed, I should have discovered him." Hardy makes it clear in the *Life* that the only God he has in mind here is the anthropomorphic one that arouses his distrust, for "It is so easy nowadays to call any force above or under the sky by the name of 'God'—and so pass as orthodox cheaply." Accordingly, he was distrustful even of other poets who seemed to find religious comfort glibly. He called the concluding solace of Tennyson's *In Memoriam* "too easily won from too little evidence";

---

2   Florence Hardy, *Life of Thomas Hardy*, p. 285.

he derided Browning's verse as "comfortably unaware" of what Shelley called "Victorious Wrong" and Sophocles "the vast injustice of the gods"; and he ridiculed Arnold's defense of religious dogma as "hair-splitting."

But there was considerable emotional ambivalence in Hardy's sense of the Christian religious tradition that had fed his young imagination. At times it is evoked with tenderness—when it is associated with childhood or the past or Christmas, as in the charming early novel *Under the Greenwood Tree* or in the well-known poem "The Oxen." In the *Life*, Hardy went so far as to say (somewhat tongue in cheek but not without a measure of sincerity): "although invidious critics had cast slurs upon him as [Agnostic, Atheist, or pessimist] they had never thought of calling him what they might have called him much more plausibly—'churchy'—not in any intellectual sense, but insofar as instincts and emotions ruled." In one poem, "God's Funeral," the speaker regrets he cannot buoy the faith of those who mourn God's death, admitting, "what was mourned for, I, too, long had prized." Another, "The Impercipient," pictures the speaker sitting unresponsively in church, suggesting weakened feelings toward religious tradition. The comic "Respectable Burgher" responds to the Higher Criticism's approach to the Bible neither with satisfaction nor dismay but with something like ironic bemusement. And a similar ambivalence marks "Drinking Song" whose rollicking devil-may-care refrains describe Darwin's idea that we are one with creeping things as one of those great thoughts that *diminishes* the world. Hardy's unbelief, tinged with the residue of belief, sometimes admits nostalgia but often finds that sentiment too weak to express his dismay, and takes on a bitter edge as a result.

About the mature novels, critics have commonly remarked that Hardy honors a pagan life-acceptance and discovers an "ache" in the minds of characters exposed to modernism. Christian morality in his two strongest novels, *Tess of the D'Urbervilles* and *Jude the Obscure* is presented as relentlessly oppressive, especially in regard to sex and marriage. Their two protagonists become critics of this morality. One remembers Tess, with the infant she had hardly wanted, coming across painted inscriptions like THY, DAMNATION, SLUMBERETH, NOT and telling the artisan, "I think they are horrible...crushing! Killing!" Jude similarly turns on his beloved Sue, after she so painfully reverts:

> "We must conform!" she said mournfully. "All the ancient wrath of the Power above us has been vented upon us...It is no use fighting against God!" "It is only against man and senseless circumstance," said Jude.

A number of poems, while *telling* us that God is no more than a blind and inhuman force, *show* us this force. The various deific epithets are more or less unflattering—"purblind Doomsters," "Vast Imbecility," "Great Face behind," "Immanent Will," "Spinner of Years"—but they elicit an emotional response. Though hardly comforting, Hardy's God is speaking to us. A number of poems ("Nature's Questioning," "The Mother Mourns," "God-Forgotten," "By the Earth's Corpse," "A Dream Question," "A Plaint to Man") depict God or his proxy Nature as not unmindful of human suffering but unable or unwilling to relieve it. When conscientiousness prompts Hardy to introduce a meliorist sentiment, his deity becomes abstract. The Spirit of the Years (in *The Dynasts*) describes this power as "A Will that wills above the will of each,/ Yet but the will of all conjunctively."[3]

Hardy's art seeks to give us some felt sense of what is adversarial to man and thus to account for the pain inherent in the human situation. In "Hap" the purblind doomsters are not really neutral as the word hap implies, but mischievous. The Spinner of Years in "The Convergence of the Twain" relishes arranging the Titanic's collision with the iceberg. The God of "Channel Firing" reveals several emotions toward the awakened dead: dismay at man's ongoing folly, pleasure in the prospect of a punishing Judgment Day, pity for man's need of rest (this in parenthesis), and a final indifference to the whole show. In other poems the God figure doesn't remember the creation or claims he didn't expect men to become so conscious and hence critical of his acts or is represented by proxies ("Nature's Questioning," "The Subalterns") whose very bewilderment only underlines the sorrow of man's frustrated spiritual desire.

That Hardy is earnest about all this despite the playful ironies is shown by his persistent effort to take a meliorist rather than pessimist line. In some poems he suggests that the Unconscious Will of the universe is growing aware of itself, is developing a providential purpose. This idea is given emphasis in the final Chorus of his most ambitious poem, *The Dynasts*:

> But—a stirring thrills the air
> Like to sounds of joyance there
> That the rages
> Of the ages

---

3 Hynes, ed., *Thomas Hardy: The Complete Poetical Works*, vol 5, Part Third, I:v: 31.

Shall be cancelled, and deliverance offered from the darts that were,
Consciousness the Will informing, till it fashion all things fair!

Other especially earnest meliorist sentiments are found in poems titled "The Sleep-Worker" and "Agnosto Theo" (To an Unknown God). The latter envisions a "Willer masked and dumb" that will grow percipient and mend the human scene so that we may discern "wrong/Dying as of self-slaughter, whereat I/ Would raise my voice in song."[4]

But, although it sometimes achieves eloquence, the meliorist sentiment tends to run against the grain of the writer's temperament. To counter the charge of pessimism, Hardy liked to quote his own line from "In Tenebris II"—"If way to the Better there be, it exacts a full look at the Worst"—but such a sensible view of the matter doesn't explain why we judge his pessimism to be *characteristic*. In the "General Preface to the Wessex Edition of 1912," Hardy *did* adequately account for this bias, telling us that "differing natures find their tongue in the presence of differing spectacles. Some natures become vocal at tragedy, some are made vocal by comedy, and it seems to me that to whichever of these aspects of life a writer's instinct for expression more readily responds, to that he should allow it to respond." We must, I think, agree with Martin Seymour-Smith that Hardy's "notions of meliorism are reluctant and confused defences against attacks on him," which, however, testify to his "instinctive decency."

---

4 Along with these passages from his poetry, Hardy's fullest prose statement of his meliorist sympathies is found in the "Apology" to "Late Lyrics and Earlier," in Gibson ed., *Complete Poems*, pp. 256-62. His earnestness about meliorism is evident also in passages of the *Life* (pp. 335, 387, 449, 454). But he is said to have regretted writing the upbeat close of *The Dynasts* when World War broke out.

A more useful question than the source of Hardy's pessimism is why, given the degree to which the writer arranges misfortune for the living beings imaged in his poems and novels, these beings are far from being puppets. The answer is surely his extraordinary empathy with suffering, both powerful and intimate. The "aged thrush," frail, gaunt and small," that sings joyfully in so incongruous a landscape, is empowered by the poet's will and does not seem frail at all. The same is true of "the last chrysanthemum," a poignant image of belatedness and isolation but also of endurance and tenacity. A Blinded Bird is readymade for sentimental treatment, but Hardy's poem using that phrase as a title ends defiantly: "Who is divine? This bird." Shelley's Skylark, whose descendant was sighted in Rome, is after all just a poor mortal bird—but to have (however indirectly) inspired such a poem, what a bird! It is true that Hardy tends to dwarf the numerous notables that populate his epic-drama, *The Dynasts*, although Kenneth Millard has shown that it is possible to make discriminations among them (the English less dwarfed than the French), but the familiar brooding pity for humanity and the mordant irony concerning man's relation to the Overworld are still evident in what Millard himself takes to be the work's central dialogue, that between the Spirit of the Pities on the one hand the Spirits Sinister and Ironic on the other.[5]

Hardy's sufferers are stoic. They do not surrender to despair any more than they successfully surmount it. Margaret Mahar brings out this idea subtly in her commentary on Hardy's fine and famous poem, "During Wind and Rain." The "Ah, no" refrain seems at first simply to cancel out each happy seasonal image, mocking a lilting rhythm with a harsh final line that suggests the

---

5 Seymour-Smith, "Introduction" to *Mayor of Casterbridge*, p. 16.

futility of all human endeavor. But the overall logic is not so simple. Mahar places the poem against Shelley's "Ode to the West Wind" from which it derives. To Shelley's final question ("If Winter comes, can Spring be far behind?") "During Wind and Rain" answers: "both behind and ahead. Hardy affirms the cyclical state of things as they are, and that affirmation is neither quite acquiescence nor a springboard to transcendence." In his typical lyrics, Mahar generalizes, past and present are related as equals rather than in terms of cause and effect because Hardy thinks of the present not as fulfilling the past but repeating it.[6]

Is there a similar logic at work in the novels despite the fact that narrative depends on linear progression? I think there is. Plot in the great novels, *Tess* and *Jude*, does not so much unfold as accrete. Irving Howe observed with particular reference to *Jude* that what we remember of the novel are its moments rather than the sequence of events.[7] Only in *The Mayor of Casterbridge* does the tragic conclusion unfold progressively, following inevitably from the character of the protagonist. It is therefore properly judged to be the most neatly structured of the late, great novels.

Plot in Hardy's novels often functions as an agent of the Immanent Will, exploiting coincidence or whatever device comes to hand in order to secure the protagonist's destruction. His addition of "finished his sport with Tess" to Aeschylus's august phrase "President of the Immortals" is only the most notorious evidence of this will to destruction. So the most interesting question about *Tess* is why the heroine's character remains so powerfully present.

---

6 Mahar, "Hardy's Poetry of Renunciation," in Bloom (ed.). *Thomas Hardy*, pp. 164ff.

7 Howe, *Thomas Hardy*, p. 145.

Hardy's imagination was at least as much invested in the sentient sufferer as in the opposing force of fate, and the result in the case of Tess is uncanny. Her sensuous presence on the page, as D. H. Lawrence among others perceived,[8] is not just strong but palpable. For the sake of his tragedy, Hardy must make her passive enough to be vulnerable to the combination of different kinds of moral crassness embodied in Alec and Angel, but Tess herself is not flawed as an individual--or is only insofar as she embodies symbolically her family history. Nor does her character change fundamentally: she is always sensitive to suffering and injustice, and is allowed gradually to be more active in protest against them. Thus to the question raised by the narrator in the seduction scene—"why so often the coarse appropriates the finer thus, the wrong man the woman, the wrong woman the man"—the novel's answer is 'senseless circumstance' far more than individual psychology. In the cases of Angel Clare and Sue Bridehead Hardy brilliantly anticipates Freud's 'return of the repressed' as an aspect of individual psychological development. But Tess and Jude are brilliant in another way. Neither of them is deeply flawed or fundamentally changed. Jude's valedictory "Let the day perish wherein I was born" echoes Job in the midst rather than at the end of his ordeal, and Tess at Stonehenge is an image of sacrifice rather than pathos. Unlike Henchard and most tragic protagonists, neither is marked by hubris or chastened in the course of the story.

Jude is rather unconvincingly assigned character flaws—susceptibility to strong drink (like Henchard) and to women. But the sensitive boy hurt by the cruelty of nature and the coldness of man (nobody came with the promised Latin and Greek gram-

---

8 Lawrence, "Study of Thomas Hardy, *in Phoenix*, Ch IX.

mars "because nobody does") is basically the same as the courageous adult who would defy the injustice of human arrangements. Hardy himself can scarcely be said to blame Jude's character for his fate, apart from the side issue of heredity. Sue's story like Angel's could be considered tragedy—good stuff gone wrong—but Jude's like Tess' is something else.

But these are Hardy's most exceptional heroic figures, and it is important to appreciate the fact that his sympathies are often drawn to figures of lesser strength as well. Pain and suffering, to which he himself was exceptionally sympathetic, are after all universal. Elizabeth-Jane in *The Mayor of Casterbridge* does not leave upon us an indelible impression comparable to that left by Jude, Tess or her father Henchard. But there is not a more quintessential prose passage in his work—not one more intimate, honest and unsentimental—than the one in which she expresses her disappointment on learning that Donald Farfrae, the one person she thought might be her own, has transferred his affection to the very woman who is now befriending her:

> She had learnt the lesson of renunciation, and was familiar with the wreck of each day's wishes as with the diurnal setting of the sun. If her earthly career had taught her few book philosophies it had at least as well practiced her in this. Yet her experience had consisted less in a series of pure disappointments than in a series of substitutions. Continually it had happened that what she desired had not been granted her, and that what had been granted her she had not desired. So she viewed with an approach to equanimity the now cancelled days when Donald had been her undeclared lover, and wondered what unwished-for thing Heaven might send in place of him.

We should remember that Elizabeth-Jane is destined in her story to reclaim her Donald after all, so what is at issue here is not Hardy's will to pessimism as much as his sensitivity to loss.

For Hardy as for other Victorian writers, God was dying or disappearing, a not yet completed process. For Wallace Stevens a generation later, the disappearance of God is an accomplished fact, and for Samuel Beckett, a generation after that, his permanent absence is a source of mordant humor. Hardy was born early enough to be more than a little impressed by the deterministic theories, rationalist and irrationalist, that he found in Darwin and Schopenhauer. He wished to show human beings not at ease with the unconscious will of the world. His imagination was drawn both by the tyranny of this force and by the stoic courage of the sufferer.

His pessimism bothered earlier readers rather more than it does today because many felt he was depriving them of some comfort that they needed to live their lives. We have since become able to see this same pessimism more positively, as an admission of pain that bravely refuses to be allayed in traditional ways. His antitheism is derived from the fact that he believed the pain of existence to be irremediable, and in part he was attracted to the views of Darwinists and of Schopenhauer because of their very frankness in this regard. Hardy was seeking through poetry and fiction, and even through science and philosophy, a vision severe enough to acknowledge that, as he phrases it in the *Life*, "Pain has been, and pain is."[9]

---

9   *Life of Thomas Hardy*, p. 35.

The Need to Believe:
Wallace Stevens' Elegant Antitheism

The word God was congenial to Stevens. It was "the major poetic idea in the world," the major myth. Negatively this means it was "merely a poetic idea"; positively it means "God and the imagination are one."[1] Stevens leaves no doubt as to the relative importance for him of the literal and poetic meanings of the word: "We no longer think that God was, but was imagined."[2] The word was valuable to him because it was rich in resonance, able to infuse the word Imagination with "nobility" and "elegance." His bias was always and emphatically aesthetic.

Although not a religious believer, Stevens did have what might be called a religious sensibility. He was devout in his attentions to the physical world and to his feelings about what he saw and heard in nature, and he said things like: "[Poets] purge themselves before reality...in what they intend to be saintly exercises."[3] Or, again, "My own way out toward the future involves a confidence in the spiritual role of the poet... in restoring to the imagination what it is losing at such a catastrophic pace."[4] Not surpris-

---

1 Stevens, *Collected Poetry & Prose*, pp. 674, 914.
2 Stevens, *Letters*, p. 369.
3 Stevens, *Collected Poetry & Prose*, p. 790.
4 Stevens, *Letters*, p. 340.

ingly, he rejected the label of atheist, which must have seemed bleakly rationalistic. He was seeking a humanism of an expansive type—Emersonian, Whitmanian, Nietzschean—one that, without committing him to transcendence, was responsive to the suggestiveness of a word like "beyond". The poet asks the muse of Fictive Music for the power to express what is "near" but "not too near," "like" but "not too like," the human. Meditating on "the man with the blue guitar, the poet would make a song "of" ourselves yet "beyond us." The singer who creates an idea of order at Key West mediates between her human audience and the "inhuman" ocean.

Stevens' stance, then, extends the idea of humanism, but it is naturalistic from beginning to end. "Divinity must live within herself" he writes of the woman whose spiritual need serves as a foil "Sunday Morning." "God is in me or else is not at all," he states in a collection of aphorisms ("Adagia II"). Religion's myth of heaven is mocked in some poems ("The Worms at Heaven's Gate," "Cortège for Rosenbloom"), dismissed as "colossal illusion" in another ("Landscape with Boat") or, in an "Adagia" aphorism, put aside as "an exhausted culture" unable to produce poetic power. We cannot go back to a religious age, Stevens everywhere assumes, even though our disbelief (and a poet, he said, inevitably shares the disbelief of his times) may trouble us. Unlike such last-gasp Victorian doubters as Twain and Hardy, Stevens takes a position firmly beyond any debate about the presence of God. For him, "loss of faith… is growth."[5] What remains is the need to believe.

The belief that Stevens cherished most deeply was that poetry could "take the place/ Of empty heaven and its hymns."[6] In

---

5 Stevens, *Collected Poetry & Prose*, p. 911.
6 *Ibid.*, p. 137.

another wording, "After one has abandoned a belief in god, poetry is that essence which takes its place as life's redemption."[7] But Stevens insists on calling what so ardently held his imagination a fiction, albeit a supreme fiction. "The final belief is to believe in a fiction, which you know to be a fiction."[8]

We can best gauge the distinctiveness of his thought here if we ask how his idea of believing in a fiction differs from, even as it resembles, similar thinking on the part of the two thinkers who most directly influenced this aspect of his work, William James and George Santayana. In *The Will to Believe* published in 1897, a book much discussed during Stevens' Harvard years, James was at pains to defend the *right* to believe against the aggressive agnosticism of writers like T. H. Huxley and W. K. Clifford. Although not himself religious, James was convinced that believing was psychologically and morally advantageous, and so argued that one could and should adopt belief as hypothesis in the same way that a scientist adopts hypothesis as an investigative tool. Stevens alludes to James's title phrase in a letter written years later, with a slight but significant change, altering the word "will" to "need." "Underlying my poem ('Notes toward a Supreme Fiction') is the idea that...it might be possible to believe in something that we know to be untrue. Of course we do that every day, but we don't make the most of the fact that we do it out of the need to believe, what in your day, and mine, in Cambridge was called the will to believe."[9] James himself would have found strange the idea of believing in a declared fiction. For him, a hypothesis, unlike a fiction, *may be true*, and that possibility was

---

7 *Ibid.*, p. 901.
8 *Ibid.* p. 903.
9 Stevens, *Letters*, p. 443.

important. He wanted to argue the case for religious belief on grounds that would make sense to a scientist or philosopher, not to a poet whose need to believe could be satisfied by poems.

Stevens' idea of believing in a fiction is closer in spirit to Santayana's linking of religion and poetry than to James's linking of religion and science. In *Interpretations of Poetry and Religion* (1900) Santayana had written: "religion and poetry are identical in essence [and] differ merely in the way they are attached to practical affairs." Like Stevens, he considered the Christian mythology exhausted, but he was still seeking poetry *in* religion rather than *instead of* it, which was perhaps why Stevens, who knew Santayana at Harvard and always admired him, shied away from nominating him for a projected academic Chair in Poetry. More subtly, it may be why, in his tribute poem, "To an Old Philosopher in Rome," Stevens, in Harold Bloom's words, "for once allowed himself to repress his strong awareness that the mind could never be satisfied."[10]

Perhaps the closest analogue to Stevens' idea of believing in a fiction is to be found in the idea of "literary belief" proposed by his fellow-poet Robert Frost. As Frost put it, poems are "believed into existence, [beginning] in something more felt than known." For both Stevens and Frost writing poems entailed an emotional commitment that, though temporary, was total at the moment. Both knew well that, in Frost's words, "if you don't believe in poetry, you cannot write it."[11] Stevens knew, like Nietzsche, and perhaps picked up the idea from him, that fiction can have a strong truth value for the creative mind. One striking way he

---

10 Bloom, *Wallace Stevens*, p. 363.
11 Frost "Education by Poetry: A Meditative Monologue," in *Robert Frost: Poetry and Prose*, pp. 332-33, 338-39.

expressed this was: "We never arrive intellectually. But emotionally we arrive constantly."[12] "Thought is false happiness" (a phrase from the poem "Crude Foyer") was another phrasing of the idea, a statement that would not have won the assent of James or Santayana.

Stevens emphasized the role of emotional mobility in the making of poems, which means that a poem's implicit thinking is an activity, a moving between poles. His favorite names for these poles were Reality and the Imagination. Reality he understood as the succession of appearances given to the mind's eye, and Imagination as the making of metaphor out of this material. Stevens can collapse the distinction between them at any time, as when he writes in "Adagia": "Reality is an Activity of the Most August Imagination" or "Things seen are things as seen." But he wants to think of them as persisting contraries because he values the pressure that each source—the given world and the made world, the perceived and the perceiver—exerts on the other.

This dialectic is set into motion by what Frank Kermode called "the urgency of need" and Helen Vendler "passionate feeling."[13] The mobility of the poet's mind was further responsive to a range of moods, often expressed by seasonal symbolism. In a summery mood the pressure exerted by Imagination was ascendant, in a wintry mood the pressure of Reality dominated, but Stevens was always aware of the danger of thinking in such a way that one pole loses touch with the other. "Sometimes I believe most in the imagination for a long time and then, without reasoning about it, turn to reality and believe in that and that alone. But both of

---

12 Stevens, *Collected Poetry & Prose*, p. 911.
13 Kermode, p. 27; Vendler, p.10.

these things project themselves endlessly and I want them to do just that."[14]

Of course moods, states of mind, vary not only back and forth in the short run but also in discernible tendencies over a lifetime. In Stevens' case the arc of longer change is noteworthy. Simplifying only a little, one can say that his poetic output breaks into three periods. The first consists of the poems written up to about age 40 and collected in *Harmonium* (1923), a volume that vaulted its author at once into poetic fame. Despite some melancholy undercurrents, most of the poems in the volume are exuberant, sensuous, sparkling, intellectually playful or teasingly difficult, elegant and eloquent. In light of my antitheistic emphasis, the most important and representative of these poems is "Sunday Morning," which looks now as if it had been written in response to a challenge posed later in one of Stevens' own essays, "Imagination as Value": "The great poems of heaven and hell have been written and the great poem of the earth remains to be written."

After an unusual ten year hiatus, Stevens adopted a more sober and analytic idiom for the poems of his middle years, which includes the Second World War period. Two major poems from this period that I want to touch on are "Notes toward a Supreme Fiction" and "Esthétique du Mal," which analyze in a poetic idiom his idea of believing in a fiction, and address as well, if more obliquely, the status of poetry (especially of a poetry like his own, perceived by his readers as removed from the gritty social and political scene) in a time of social crisis.

The argument of "Notes toward a Supreme Fiction" is developed in a sequence of three headings: "It Must Be Abstract," It Must Change," "It Must Give Pleasure." Through the word "ab-

---

14 Stevens, *Letters*, p. 710.

stract," Stevens suggests that he wants to get behind poetry itself and find its initiating energy. In the physical world this fount and origin would be "the sun," which, as the section's cardinal image, becomes equivalent to something like the mind's originating warmth and spark, the fount of all making. "It Must Change" implies that the creative imagination is necessarily mobile, shuttling between those poles of Reality and Imagination. And "It Must Give Pleasure" warns against the danger of getting stuck at either end, the danger of a fixed belief, as in religious or political doctrines. The "Coda" that Stevens adds, though not especially convincing, is significant because it implicitly acknowledges the fact that poetry in a time of war may be perceived as a superfluous luxury. It begins by linking his poetic world, so concerned with the specialized idea of believing a fiction, with the anxious world around him, declaring that there will always be "war" between "the mind and sky," But, as if admitting that this bridging is an insufficient argument for relevance, it then, more boldly, introduces the image of a dying soldier. An earlier poem, "The Death of a Soldier" had described such a death as "absolute and without memorial," and Stevens, in modifying that harsh truth here, is not about to soften it with any of the standard consolations. But it is none the less true, the poem attempts to say, that "proper words," the poet's forte, may contribute something, may enable the soldier to "die gladly if he must."

"Esthétique du Mal" (1944) tries another, more poetically fruitful tack, asking what is the role of the poet in a world where reality is so hostile to the imagination that "one's desire/ Is too difficult to tell from despair." Can poetry be made of such negation? Stevens acknowledges that evil has become in our day more difficult to imagine ("The death of Satan was a tragedy/ For the imagination") and does not attempt to address what most readers would consider recognizable evils. But he turns the very image of impoverishment into an opportunity: "The greatest poverty is not to live/ In a physical world, to feel that our desire/ Is too difficult to tell from despair." This way of stating the situation sparks a renewal of belief in the power of poetry and a corresponding eloquence:

> One might have thought of sight, but who could think
> Of what it sees, for all the ill it sees?....
> And out of what one sees and hears and out
> Of what one feels, who could have thought to make
> So many selves, so many sensuous worlds,
> As if the air, the mid-day air, was swarming
> With the metaphysical changes that occur,
> Merely in living as and where we live.

In Stevens' third and last phase, wintry moods become dominant, which means not that Imagination quite yields to Reality but that its role becomes more subtle, and some critics have come to prefer this late "wintry" style to the gaudy Stevens of *Harmonium*. Helen Vendler, one of those critics, goes so far as to call "the disappointment of desire" "the fundamental donnée" of the poet's work. In "The Course of a Particular" (according to Vendler the poem he was born to write), the human meaning of the repeated "cry of the leaves" diminishes to point zero: "until, at last, the cry concerns no one at all." Yet the cry itself lingers in our minds, so it is possible to say that the poet has successfully imagined "no one at all." Another admirable poem from the late period, "Final Soliloquy of the Interior Paramour," consoles us with the knowledge of what is enough, finding comfort in an image of our diminishment: "Out of all the indifferences, into one thing...a single shawl/ Wrapped tightly round us, since we are poor."

The late poem that to my mind most subtly connects the contraries while conveying the wintry spirit is "Of Mere Being," which concludes the *Collected Poems*.

> The palm at the end of the mind,
> Beyond the last thought, rises
> In the bronze décor.
>
> A gold-feathered bird
> Sings in the palm, without human meaning,
> Without human feeling, a foreign song.
>
> You know then that it is not the reason
> That makes us happy or unhappy.
> The bird sings. Its feathers shine.
>
> The palm stands on the edge of space.
> The wind moves slowly in the branches.
> The bird's fire-fangled feathers dangle down.

Gold coloring, palm, bird, and fire are familiar images in Stevens, evoking desire in its more youthful manifestations. But the poem is seeking the end of desire, the mereness of being. The bird sings, the palm stands, the wind moves. And the last line captures one last gaudy flourish, "fire-fangled-feathers," then checks it by another alliteration suggestive of sexual finality, "dangles down." Stevens' "mere being" with its absence of human meaning contains no hint of transcendence, protest, or even acquiescence. Yet it moves us by extending our sense of the human into the space of the inhuman. The absence of human feeling in the bird's song (second tercet) means that this song itself cannot be the cause of our emotions (third tercet), but, as the concluding tercet implies, our *capacity* to see and hear the bird is still connected to *what* is seen and heard. The source of feeling springs from within the self, hence it is human feeling that has made this connection. The poem shows that it endures after all. In his essay "Relations between Poetry & Painting" Stevens wrote: "Imagination is not so much an aspect of humanism as it is "a vital self-assertion in a world in which nothing but the self remains."

How then shall we say that this poet, who in his elegant way firmly puts aside any traditional theism, satisfies his need to believe? It is not quite enough or even quite right to say that he believes in poems and poetry. What becomes clear as we reflect on Stevens is that the true grail of his quest is the power that *went into* the making of poems, and this must be the same human power that once went into the making of "God." Frank Kermode had it exactly right when he wrote: "In the end that is the subject of Stevens: living without God and finding it good, because of the survival of the power that once made Him suffice."

Samuel Beckett and the Bastard
Who Doesn't Exist

Beckett found his audience with *Waiting for Godot*, written in 1948-49, published in 1952, and first produced in Paris in 1953, the US in 1954, and the UK in 1955. Somewhat unfortunately, the moment coincided with the emergence of a fashion (lasting about fifteen years) for Death of God theology, and so a play that deliberately avoided specification and that maximized uncertainty was subjected to allegorical interpretation.[1] Those hungry for moral significance were of course not satisfied by the author's insistence that he himself did not know who or what Godot was or even if he existed.[2]

But a teasing name like Godot cannot simply be ignored, especially in view of the publication, in 1943, a few years before the play was composed, of Simone Weil's *Attente de Dieu*, translated

---

1   One little example of how Beckett maximized uncertainty may stand for others. In Matthew 25:33-34 Jesus implies that the virtuous "sheep" will be blessed while the vicious "goats" will not be. But the Boy in Beckett's play reports that Mr. Godot beats his brother who minds the *sheep* but not himself who minds the *goats*. Our attempt to make a meaningful inference from this report is thus baffled.

2   Beckett answered a question from one correspondent as follows:"I do not know who Godot is. I do not even know if he exists. And I do not know if they believe he does or not, those two who are waiting for him." (See *The New Yorker Magazine* (24 June and 1 July, 1996), p. 136. Similarly, his director Alan Schneider reported (in the *Chelsea Review*, Autumn 1958) that Beckett had told him:"If I knew [who or what Godot is] I would have said so in the play." Quoted by Duckworth, p. xxv.

as *Waiting for God*. In fact the name is a typical Beckettian tease of the 1940s, like Mr Knott in *Watt* or Moran's boss Youdi, names that have been rightly taken by critics to be mock versions of Not and Yahweh. The *ot* suffix serves to ridicule the honored name it suggests, the way Molloy's addition of the letter g to "Ma" "abolished" and "spat" on a name that ought to be honored.

In his magisterial biography *Damned to Fame*, James Knowlson describes Beckett as an agnostic.[3] This makes sense because the oeuvre thematizes not knowing. But, if agnosticism implies positive skepticism regarding the existence God, it is not quite accurate. As Porter Abbott argues, Beckettian skepticism actually requires a "metaphysical openendedness" expressing "a fascination with possibilities" rather than an absolute skepticism.[4] Beckett's "antitheism," as I would call it, is *neither* the agnostic's positive skepticism *nor* the atheist's positive denial of God's existence but a characteristic imaginative movement whereby theological and religious allusions are evoked and then turned in a subversively ironic direction. And such allusions abound in his work. As he told Colin Duckworth, "Christianity is a mythology with which I am perfectly familiar, so I make use of it."[5] Make use of it he did, for these allusions are almost always occasions for irreverent wit.

It is important to understand that Beckett's satirical wit at the expense of the Christian religion is characteristically aggressive. The intention is not merely to scale down the comforts and consolations of faith but to puncture them as a cheat and a delusion. Trying to keep Beckett at least marginally within the Christian

---

3   Knowlson, *passim*.
4   Abbott, *Beckett Writing* Beckett, pp. 55, 183.
5   Quoted in Bryden, p. 35.

fold, the critic Mary Bryden comments, "Even when repeatedly stamped upon the *idea* of a Godhead keeps growing back in Beckett's texts."⁶ It would be more accurate to reverse these clauses and say, even though the idea of God keeps growing back in Beckett's texts, it is repeatedly stamped upon. This does not mean that Beckett wants to define himself as outside of Christian tradition. As Shira Wolosky acutely observed, "Beckett does not work so much within or out of theological tradition as reflect back upon it."⁷

Beckett's wit requires that God's existence be in some way postulated so that it can be attacked, much the way a bowling pin must be set up in order to be knocked down. A quintessential example is Hamm's bitter comment when he and his little group in *Endgame* must abandon their prayerful attitude as fruitless: "The bastard! He doesn't exist!" The denial of God's existence is witty because, combined with the personifying word "bastard," it is illogical, but this very illogic reveals its cutting, passionate force. This is emotional repudiation, not intellectual argument. No wonder that, when the Lord Chamberlain wanted "the bastard" removed while allowing the atheistic (but by itself rather dull) little sentence to stand, Beckett dug in his heels, writing to his director, Alan Schneider, "He doesn't exist without 'the bastard' is inacceptable [sic] to me."⁸

---

6   Bryden, p. 1.
7   Wolosky, *Language Mysticism*, p. 93.
8   Quoted by Dan Gunn, "The beam of Sam's light." *Times Literary Supplement* (15 January 1999), p. 4. To appreciate the sharpness of Beckett's wit, one might compare it to similar but less keen attempts by Prosper Merimée and the Marquis De Sade. Merimée wrote: "His only excuse is that He doesn't exist." And Sade: "I wish that for a moment you could exist/ To have the pleasure better to insult you."

His target is not Christianity as such but any deceptive spiritual comfort—which, to be sure, Christianity and other religions offer and advertise as stock in trade. For this enemy of false consolation, a phrase like "first love" (the title he gave to a cynical story) or like "joy forever" is irritating. Youdi's messenger alters Keats's famous line to "life is a thing of beauty and a joy forever" so that Moran can deliver the punch: "do you think he meant human life?" "The Lord upholdeth all that fall" declared the biblical psalmist, but the bitter humor of the radio play titled "All That Fall" exposes not the Bible as such but our readiness to hope that its language can still support us.

It helps to keep in mind this larger target when we encounter this author's theological allusions. One example of such ironic allusion is the triad "incorruptible, uninjurable, unchangeable," St. Augustine's attributions for God applied to Belaqua's rather more dubious love object, the Smeraldina of *Dream of Fair to Middling Women*. Another is, "And now abideth these three: Doubt, Despair & Scrounging" (from the *Dream* notebook). And still another is, "apathia, athambia, aphasia" (from Lucky's tirade). The first two words, in this case, are traditional terms employed in so-called negative theology; they are grouped discordantly with another word, "aphasia," a psychiatric term denoting the inability to speak or understand. Some critics have taken "aphasia" to mean merely "not answering prayers,"[9] but this keeps the terms on the same plane and spoils the wit. Mary Bryden comments nicely: "A sometimes searing awareness of different or sundered planes is for Beckett infinitely preferable to a... reassuring syn-

---

9 Duckworth, for example, p. cvii

thesis of them. Hence his distaste the fluidity of the Ich-Gott relation in Rilke's poetry."[10]

The sharpness of Beckett's antitheism comes across vividly when we compare his use of the Augustinian phrase "honey of heaven" with Wallace Stevens' use of it. In "Le Monocle de Mon Oncle" Stevens wrote that "the honey of heaven may or may not come," a politely skeptical sentence because the poet's loyalty is clearly to the honey "of earth [that] comes and goes at once." Beckett, on the other hand, jumps all over the phrase. Augustine had described his pre-conversion self, in Book 9 of the *Confessions*, as "a pestilent person, a bitter and a blind bawler against those writings which are honied with the honey of heaven." Beckett copied this along with other quotations from the book and interjected irritably, "against the honey what honey bloody well you know the honey." And, still irritated, in *Dream of Fair to Middling Women* he twice uses the word "honey" in connection with Belacqua and Alba, and twice turns on it to say, "What honey?" The solacing sweetness of the phrase "honey of heaven," rather than Christianity itself, could not be tolerated.

Beckett saw the human situation not in terms of faith, hope and charity but in terms of suffering, which means, perhaps paradoxically, that there was one Christian image that he actually welcomed and exploited—crucifixion. Making use of the possibilities in this case required him to shift the ironic strategy, and show that a *painful* Christian image was not painful *enough*. Now the point was to show that the horror of Christ's crucifixion can be overmatched in everyday experience by the "suffering of being," a key phrase in Beckett's early monograph on Proust. Creating a kind of black humor, the wit now suggests that crucifixion

---

10 Bryden, p. 22

might be thought of as an easy way out of this suffering. Estragon has only the vaguest recollection of the Bible, is bewildered by notions of repentance, sin and salvation, but he understands punishment very well indeed and readily identifies with Christ as fellow sufferer—"All my life I've compared myself to him"—though of course Christ's suffering in a land where "they crucified quick" was merciful compared to his own lifelong crucifixion. Molloy, similarly, describes his painful progress on crutches as "a veritable calvary, with no limit to its stations and no hope of crucifixion." ("No hope of crucifixion" is a wonderful touch.) Clov begins *Endgame* with an allusion to words spoken by Christ on the Cross: "It is finished." But, remembering his own situation, he backs off from this formulation as too comforting: "Finished, it's finished, nearly finished, it must be nearly finished....I can't be punished any more."

It has been said, notably by Georg Lukàcs, that Beckett's work is unable to protest against social injustice.[11] Theodor Adorno has rebutted the charge adroitly by indicating that Beckett's work paradoxically enables a more just society by the very thoroughness of his disengagement from the existing one, the strength of his negation compelling rather than merely asking for a change of attitude.[12] Adorno's argument is subtle and debatable but has the merit of calling attention to Beckett's by no means inert political consciousness. Pictures of cruelty and bullying pervade his work. What obscures our perception of this fact is less the lack of social reference than the writer's unwillingness to *explain* brutality (for example the why and wherefore of the "they" who beat Estragon overnight), as if he would say, in Bryden's words, "bru-

---

11 Lukàcs, *passim*.
12 Adorno, pp. 314-15.

tality...simply happens."¹³ In all the drafts of *Godot* up until the last, Beckett's name for Estragon was Lévy, a clear indication that he was thinking of his Jewish friends recently killed by the Nazis but also that he wanted, finally, not to say this in the play for the sake of universalizing his theme. In Hamm's stark words, "you're on earth, there's no cure for that!" Abbott's analysis goes to the heart of the matter:

> From beginning to end, Beckett's art is one long protest. It is written out of a horror of human wretchedness and a yearning that this wretchedness be lessened. But the overriding sense in Beckett is not that there is something wrong with society...but something massively wrong with the entire arrangement, from birth to death. Beckett's social protest is always shadowed by his metaphysical bafflement.¹⁴

This account of the matter alerts us to a danger and an opportunity in Beckett's use of the idea of God. Since the artist does not really seek to stamp *out* the idea, he has to be careful, at the risk of seeming to air a grievance, that the sufferings of his characters do not appear to derive from supernatural malevolence. Perhaps in one minor instance, the mime play attacked to *Endgame*, does he yield to this temptation—at any rate I cannot disassociate the frustrations of the figure on stage from a sadistic agency manipulating them from behind the scene. But Beckett regularly succeeds in eluding and indeed capitalizing on this danger because of his uncanny art of deflecting emotion. That is, fragments of memory rich in pathos are drawn up into a more neutral experience in present time; the emotion is there but de-

---

13 Bryden, p. 139.
14 Abbott, 147

flected by the formal displacement.[15] In this way, an incipient grievance against God expressed through Winnie (*Happy Days*), Mouth (*Not I*) or the Rooneys (*All That Fall*) is laced with humor and transformed.

Nietzsche mused marvelously: "I am afraid we are not getting rid of God because we still believe in grammar." Beckett is one of the few writers who come close to undermining that faith. He has done so mainly in two ways. One is by undoing the masterplot involving a progressive action moving to a significant close, an aspect of the broader masterplot of origins and destinies. *Waiting for Godot*, for example, shows human beings in a state of waiting without beginning or end, and even folds a traditional plot, Pozzo's fall from high to low degree, inside of this "action." A second way is by undermining our belief in an essential self made in the image of God, and this the art does by its strenuous and unavailing effort (not only in *The Unnamable*) to find a pronoun equivalent to the self. Beckett's speakers feel keenly that they have never been entirely *there*, never entirely *born*, and thus unable to become identical to themselves. They are distressingly trapped in language, and so their dream of a definitive beginning or end can never be realized.

The latter problem reminds us of what a number of philosophers have been saying, most notably Jacques Derrida. But the resemblance between Beckett and Derrida on this matter entails an important difference. Derrida relishes the infinite play of language, considering it mere illusion or nostalgia to imagine an escape from it. One of the most impassioned ideas in Beckett's work, however, is the desirability of the silence or peace of nothingness that *is* imagined as existing before or beyond language.

---

15 Abbott develops this idea, p. 29

(He once advised a critic who wished to write about his work to start from two of his favorite quotations: Democritus' "Nothing is more real than nothing" and the Descartes disciple Arnold Geulincx's "Where you are worth nothing there you do want nothing."[16]) Beckett *knows* that the dream is illusory, but his art energetically bends every resource of language to reach the unreachable. Perhaps this contrast with Derrida demonstrates that the artist has an advantage over the philosopher, even a philosopher who works in the area between philosophy and literature. Beckett can be indifferent to logical consistency, giving his conflict of emotions full expression, but Derrida is working in a mode that does not quite give him this freedom.

It has proved difficult for many readers to confront squarely Beckett's pessimism. Christopher Ricks' *Beckett's Dying Words* is a significant exception not only because of its candor but also because Ricks has the learning to show how the theme of contempt for life fits into a long and serious literary tradition.[17] Critics who want to soften it can do little more than look for wording that might be given a religious twist or stress the countervailing theme of stoicism implied, for example, by phrasing like "I can't go on, I'll go on." But Beckett has pretty thoroughly emptied out the resonance of hopeful, ever-onward sentiments. The famous "go on" at the end of *The Unnamable* is much less a program for living than for writing, for the determination to go on failing as daringly as possible in the vain hope of reaching a silence beyond words.

If we want to discover the excitement of reading Beckett we must try not to soften his "nothing" but to see that his originality

---

16 Letter to Sighle Kennedy, in Ruby Cohn, ed. *Disjecta Membra*, p. 113.
17 Ricks, *passim*

is bound up with it. His nothing is "the nourishing murk that is killing me" (as Malone puts it), where "nourishing" and "killing" are inextricably connected. In her final chapter, "Solitude, Stillness, Silence and Stars," Bryden, recognizing that Beckett privileges these images, seeks to link his art with the tradition of mysticism inherent in "negative theology." She finds that his silence is where "atheism" and "mysticism" meet.[18] But, as Shira Wolosky has strongly demonstrated, Beckett is in fact a "countermystic," negating the negative way, using the methods of negative theology to achieve different goals. When we look again at passages in his work that suggest a negative theology, we catch clearly the tone of irony—as when the Unnamable says, "First I'll say what I'm not, that's how they taught me to proceed," or as when the narrator of *Watt* asserts: "The only way one can speak of nothing is to speak of it as though it were something, just as the only way one can speak of God is to speak of him as though he were a man, which to be sure he was, in a sense, for a time, and as the only way one can speak of man...is to speak of him though he were a termite."

    The dynamic relation between negation and invention is all-important in understanding Beckett, and this has been especially well brought out by two of his interpreters. One is Porter Abbott, who shows that the more reduced Beckett's art became, the more mind-bending became its formal originality. He unpacks the double and triple loops in the short "A Piece of Monologue," showing it to be a work so intricately balanced between narrative and drama that it resembles an Escher graphic, one genre sliding back and forth into the other.[19] The other critic of note in this

---

18 Bryden, 185-86
19 Abbott, pp. 196, 156, 174, 108.

regard is Wolosky, who sees connection between negation and invention in terms of language rather than of form and effect. She cites other critics who follow the conventional idea that Beckett is exposing the inadequacy of language and seeking to attain the wordless truth beyond language. Her bolder idea is that Beckett's relentless reductions expose instead the fact that there is no human world beyond language, and that his own language is thereby asserting its success. To imply that only unspeaking can reach the truth hardly implies the inadequacy of one's language if one never ceases to speak—and speak inventively. She sums up her comprehensive analysis thus: "[Beckett's] use of negative tradition is finally ironic, presenting its paradoxically plethoric nothingness as in fact a void. His own negative modes, in contrast, convert nothingness into a fertile source of continuous imaginative effort."[20]

"No lack of void" appalled poor Estragon, but it stimulated Beckett (as it stimulated Nietzsche) to extraordinary achievement.

---

20 Wolosky, p. 134.

BIBLIOGRAPHY

DIDEROT

Anderson, Willa (1990). *Diderot's Dream*. Baltimore: Johns Hopkins University Press.

Crocker, Lester G. (ed.) (1966). *Diderot's Selected Writings*. Translated by Derek Coleman. New York: Macmillan.

Diderot, Denis (1955). *Correspondance de Diderot 1713-1757. Paris.*

_____. (1986) *Jacques the Fatalist and His* Master. Translated by Michael Henry, with an Introduction and Notes by Martin Hall. London: Penguin Books.

_____. (1966) *Rameau's Nephew/ D'Alembert's Dream*. Translated with Introductions by Leonard Tancock. London: Penguin Books.

Fellows, Otis (1989). *Diderot* (revised edition). Boston: G.K. Hall.

Furbank, P. N. (1992). *Diderot: A Critical Biography*. New York: Knopf.

Mason, John Hope (1982). *The Irrepressible Diderot*. London: Quartet Books.

Sherman, Carol (1976). *Diderot: The Art of Dialogue*. Geneva: Librairie Droz.

Stewart, J. and Kemp, J. (editors) (1937). *Diderot: Interpreter of Nature: Selected Writings*. Westport (CT.): Hyperion Press.

Stott, Rebecca. (2012). *Darwin's Ghosts: The Secret History of Evolution*. New York: Spiegel & Grau.

Vartanian, Aram (1984). "Diderot or the Dualist in Spite of Himself," in *Diderot: A Bicentennial Tribute*. Edited by Jack Urdank and Herbert Joseph. Lexington (KY): French Forum Publishers.

Wilson, Arthur M. (1972). *Diderot*. Oxford: Clarendon Press.

BÜCHNER

Benn, Maurice (1976). *The Drama of Revolt: A Critical Study of Georg Büchner*. Cambridge: Cambridge University Press.

Büchner, Georg ([1834] 1971). *Danton's Death*. Translated by Victor Price. Oxford: University Press.

Brombert, Victor (1999). *In Praise of Antiheroes: Figures and Themes in Modern European Literature: 1830-1986*. Chicago: University Press.

Hamburger, Michael (ed.) (1972). *Georg Büchner: Leonce and Lena, Lenz, Woyzeck*. Chicago: University of Chicago Press.

Hauser, Ronald (1974). *Georg Büchner*. Boston: Twayne.

Lindenberger, Herbert (1964). *Georg Büchner: Modern Critiques*. Carbondale (IL): Southern Illinois University Press.

Mueller, Carl Richard (ed.) (1963). *Büchner: Complete Plays and Prose*. New York: Hill and Wang.

NIETZSCHE

Kaufmann, Walter (1974) *Nietzsche: Philosopher, Psychologist, Antichrist*. Fourth Edition. Princeton: University Press.

_____ (1956) *Existentialism from Dostoevsky to Sartre*. Cleveland: Meridian Books.

Heidegger, Martin (1961). *Nietzsche*. Translated by David Farrell Kroll. San Francisco: Harper & Row.

Nehamas, Alexander (1985). *Nietzsche: Life as Literature*. Cambridge: Harvard University Press.

Nietzsche, Friedrich ([1872] 1967). *The Birth of Tragedy and The Case of Wagner*. Translated by Walter Kaufmann. New York: Vintage.

_____ ([1873-76] 1990). *Unmodern Observations*. Edited by William Arrowsmith. Translated by Gary Brown. New Haven: Yale University Press.

_____ ([1881] 1982). *Daybreak*. Translated by R. J. Hollingdale. Cambridge University Press.

_____ ([1882-87] 1974). *The Gay Science*. Translated by Walter Kaumann. New York: Vintage.

_____ ([1886] 1998). *Beyond Good and Evil*. Translated by Marion Faber. Oxford World Classics.

_____ ([1887]1998) *On the Genealogy of Morals*. Translated by Douglas Smith. Oxford World Classics.

_____ ([1888] 1968) *Twilight of the Idols and the Anti-Christ*. Translated by Duncan Large. Oxford World   Classics.

_____ ([1888] 1992). *Ecce Homo*. Translated by R. J. Hollingdale, Second edition. Harmondsworth: Penguin.

_____. (1968) *The Will to Power*. Translated by Walter Kaufmann and R. J. Hollingdale. New York: Vintage.

_____ ([1887] 1966) *Thus Spake Zarathustra*. Translated by Walter Kaufmann. New York: Viking.

_____ (1954-56) *Werke in drei Bänden*. Vol 3. Edited by Karl Schlecta. München: C. Hansen.

Rorty, Richard (1989). *Contingency, irony, and solidarity*. Cambridge: Cambridge University Press.

Safranski, Rüdiger (2002) *Nietzsche: A Philosophical Biography*. Translated by Shelley Frisch. New York: Norton.

Solomon, Robert C. (1986). "Nietzsche ad hominem: Perspectivism, Personality and Ressentiment," in *The Cambridge Companion to Nietzsche*. Edited by Bernd Magnus and Kathleen M. Higgins. Cambridge: Cambridge University Press.

Stack, George T. (1992) *Nietzsche and Emerson: An Elective Affinity*. Athens (OH): Ohio University Press.

TWAIN

Andrews, Kenneth R. (1950). *Nook Farm: Mark Twain's Hartford Circle*. Cambridge: Harvard University Press.

Baetzhold, Howard G. and McCullough, Joseph B. (eds.) (1995). *The Bible According to Mark Twain*. New York: Simon and Schuster.

Brodwin, Stanley (1976). "Theology of Mark Twain: Banished Adam and the Bible," in *The Mississippi Quarterly*. Vol. XXIX, No 2 (Spring).

_____ (1985). "Mark Twain in the Pulpit: The Theological Comedy of *Huckleberry Finn*," in *One Hundred Years of 'Huckleberry Finn,' The Boy, His Book, and American Culture: Centennial Essays*. Edited by Robert Sattelmeyer and J. Donald Crowley. Columbia (MO): University of Missouri Press.

_____ (1988). "Mark Twain's Theology, The Gods of a Brevet Presbyterian," in *The Cambridge Companion to Mark Twain*. Edited by Forrest G. Robinson. Cambridge: Cambridge University Press.

DeVoto, Bernard (1986) "Mark Twain and the Great Valley," in Bloom, Harold (ed.). *Mark Twain: Modern Critical Views*, New York: Chelsea Press.

_____ (ed.) (2004). *Mark Twain: Letters from the Earth: Uncensored Writings*. New York: Harper: Perennial.

Gibson, William M. (ed.) (1969). *Mark Twain's 'Mysterious Stranger' Manuscripts*. Berkeley: University of California Press.

Neider, Charles (ed.) (1975). *Autobiography of Mark Twain*. New York: Harper & Row Perennial Library.

_____ (1963). "Mark Twain's Reflections on Relligion." *The Hudson Review* (16:3).

_____ (ed.) (2005). *The Complete Short Stories of Mark Twain*. New York: Bantam Dell.

Twain, Mark (1980). *Pudd'nhead Wilson*. New York: Signet.

Whitehead, Alfred North (1933). *Adventures in Ideas*. New York: Macmillan.

Williams, James D. (1964-65). "Revision and Intention in Mark Twain's *A Connecticut Yankee*," in *American Literature*, v. 36.

HARDY

Gibson, James (ed.) (1976) *Thomas Hardy: The Complete Poems*. New York: Macmillan.

Hardy, Florence Emily (1962). *The Life of Thomas Hardy*. New York: St Martin's Press.

Hynes, Samuel (ed.) (1995). *Thomas Hardy, The Complete Poetical Works*. Oxford: Clarendon.

Howe, Irving (1967). *Thomas Hardy*. New York: Macmillan.

Lawrence, D. H. (1936). "Study of Thomas Hardy," in *Phoenix: The Posthumous Papers of D. H. Lawrence*. Edited by Edward McDonald. London: Heinemann.

Mahar, Margaret (1987). "Hardy's Poetry of Renunciation," in Harold Bloom, ed., *Thomas Hardy: Modern Critical Views*. New York: Chelsea.

Millard, Kenneth (1995) "'The Dynasts': Words... to hold the imagination," in Harold Orel, ed., *Critical Essays on Thomas Hardy's Poetry*.

Seymour-Smith, Martin (1978). "Introduction" to Thomas Hardy's *The Mayor of Casterbridge*. London: Penguin.

STEVENS

Bloom, Harold (1977). *Wallace Stevens: The Poems of Our Climate*. Ithaca NY: Cornell University Press.

Frost, Robert (1984). "Education by Poetry: A Meditative Monologue," in *Robert Frost: Poetry and Prose*, edited by Edward Connery Lathem and Lawrance Thompson. New York: Holt, Rinehart and Winston.

Kermode, Frank (1961). *Wallace Stevens*, New York: Grove Press.

Stevens, Wallace. *Collected Poetry & Prose*, edited by Frank Kermode and Joan Richardson. New York: The Library of America.

_____ (1966). *Letters of Wallace Stevens*. Edited by Holly Stevens. New York: Knopf.

Vendler, Helen (1984). *Words Chosen Out of Desire*. Knoxville (TN): University of Tennessee Press.

BECKETT

Abbott, H. Porter (1996). *Beckett Writing Beckett: The Author in the Autograph*. Ithaca (NY): Cornell University Press.

Cohn, Ruby, (ed.) (1984). *Samuel Beckett: Disjecta Membra: Miscellaneous Writing and Dramatic Fragments*. New York: Grove Press.

Adorno, Theodor (1990). "Commitment" in *The Essential Frankfurt School Reader*. Edited by. Andrew Arato and Eike Gebhardt. New York: Continuum.

Beckett, Samuel (1986). *The Complete Dramatic Works*. London: faber and faber.

_____ (1984). *Collected Shorter Prose: 1945-1980*. London: John Calder.

_____ (1965). *Three Novels*. New York: Grove Press.

_____ (1957). *Proust*. New York: Grove Press.

Bryden, Mary (1998). *Samuel Beckett and the Idea of God*. New York/ London: St. Martin's Press.

Duckworth, Colin (ed.) (1985). *Samuel Beckett: En attendant Godot*. Walton-on-Thomas (Surrey): Thomas Nelson.

Gunn, Dan (1999). 'The Beam of Sam's Light,' in *Times Literary Supplement* (15 January).

Knowlson, James (1996). *Damned to Fame: The Life of Samuel Beckett*. New York: Simon and Schuster.

Lukàcs, Georg (1962). *The Meaning of Contemporary Realism*. Translated by John Mander and Necke Mander. London: Merlin Press.

Ricks, Christopher (1993). *Beckett's Dying Words*. New York: Oxford University Press.

Wolosky, Shira. *Language Mysticism: The Negative Way of Language: Eliot, Beckett and Celan*. Stanford: Stanford University Press.

Lightning Source UK Ltd.
Milton Keynes UK
UKOW052152060213

205935UK00001B/19/P